The Confirmed Catholic's Companion

A Guide to Abundant Living

Updated Edition

Mary Kathleen Glavich, SND

saint mary's press

The Confirmed Catholic's Companion
A Guide to Abundant Living
by Mary Kathleen Glavich, SND

Edited by Nicole Kramer
Cover Design by Patricia A. Lynch
Typesetting by Complete Communications, Inc.

Cover art by Ivan Straka, used with permission of Bigstock.

The Confirmed Catholic's Companion
A Guide to Abundant Living

Dedicated with love to those for whom I have enjoyed the privilege of being a Confirmation sponsor— Lisa Marie Julia Stobierski, Julia Marie Felicity Stobierski, and Edward Frank Richard Kovacic.

Introduction: Read Me First!

Congratulations! You completed your initiation into the Catholic Church through the sacrament of Confirmation, publicly confirming your decision to be Catholic and being officially welcomed into the Church. At the first Pentecost, the Holy Spirit whooshed down upon the first disciples and filled them with faith and courage; at your Confirmation, that same Holy Spirit empowered *you* with gifts and graces to live as a Catholic—without the "wind and flames!"

As a confirmed Catholic, you have been fully inducted into a two-thousand-year-old organization that has more than a billion members around the globe—and billions more on the other side of the grave. Nearly one out of every four Americans is Catholic (seventy-eight million identify themselves as Catholics). Through the sacrament of Confirmation, you more fully joined the Communion of Saints, inheriting the privileges and responsibilities of being a Catholic follower of Jesus Christ.

So now what?

Jesus proclaimed: "I came that they may have life, and have it abundantly" (John 10:10). This book is a kind of "how to" manual to abundant living as you strive to follow the spiritual path you chose and keep the commitment you made to Jesus and the Church. Catholics are joined together in the Communion of Saints—the unity of all believers past and present, helping each other grow closer to God. This guide to abundant living brings together the prayers, practices and spiritual disciplines that many Catholics have developed and cherished over the centuries—tools for building a vibrant, personal relationship with God. You'll learn more about the Catholic faith (and *how* to learn more about it), discover an atlas for personal prayer, and realize practical tips for living out your Catholic faith 24/7.

Some practices or prayers may connect with your spirituality, others you may simply appreciate as one piece of the Catholic spiritual tradition. The Catholic faith is a rich tapestry of diverse ways of pursuing the purpose of your life: loving and being loved by the God who created and saved you. Perhaps the greatest key to abundant living is to live authentically in your personal relationship with Jesus and the Church—to look for God's fingerprints and seek them out in ways that resonate with the person God created you to be.

Occasionally, someone embarks on a quest for the secret to eternal life— you announced your discovery of that secret in the renewal of your baptismal vows during your Confirmation. Now, you can discover the secrets of living out those vows—and living them abundantly.

1. Religion: Catholic

W hat does it mean to be identified as "Catholic"? The Catholic faith is an intricate patchwork quilt of dogmas, doctrines, disciplines, traditions and spiritual wisdom—all centered around growing closer to a three-personed God who loves us relentlessly. However, to be Catholic is to be part of the Body of Christ—a family of believers who share a common mission of going "in peace to love and serve the Lord," who share a rich religious and spiritual tradition begun by Christ and continued by generations of sinners saved by grace. Part of that Catholic identity involves infusing our faith into our daily work, prayer and actions; our relationships and interactions with other people; and our commitment to serving the poor and promoting life, love and a just world.

We have big shoes (or sandals) to fill—those of Jesus. However, we also have the saints who have walked this path before us to help us along the way and teach us what they have learned—a task we also share in helping other members along. You may not have realized it, but the Catholic spiritual tradition originated even before Mary conceived Jesus, God-made-flesh, in her womb. Stories of people such as David, Moses and Esther struggling to trust God and trying to do God's will pervade the Old Testament. Through Jesus we were grafted into the Jewish tradition—a tradition that dates back to the first creation described in the Old Testament. Many of our traditions, prayers and Scripture are shared with the Jewish faith.

The daily prayer of the Jewish people is called the *Shema*: "Hear, O Israel: The Lord is our God, the Lord alone. You shall love the Lord your God with all your heart, and with all your soul, and with all your might. Keep these words I am commanding you today in your heart" (Deuteronomy 6:4-6). To this Jesus added a new commandment: "Just as I have loved you, you also

THE U. S. CATHOLIC CHURCH 2012

❖ 66.3 million Catholics (22% of the population)
❖ 38,964 priests
❖ 26,661 religious priests
❖ 17,289 permanent deacons
❖ 54,018 sisters
   4,477 brothers
❖ 30,000 lay ministers
❖ 17,644 parishes
❖ 5,636 elementary schools
   1,205 high schools
   230 colleges and universities
❖ 554 hospitals

should love one another" (John 13:35). Jesus established Catholic Christianity on that foundation. Numerous stories throughout the Gospels tell of Jesus teaching his disciples—how to live this new commandment—most prominently by his example.

After Jesus gave his life by dying on a cross, he rose from the dead and ascended into heaven—leaving behind a small but dynamic core of believers in first-century Palestine. Jesus left Peter at the helm, having consecrated him as the first pope. The apostles and Jesus' disciples passed down the lessons and tradition Jesus instilled in them, generation after generation. The Catholic Church grew until in 313 A.D. it was recognized as a religion in the Roman Empire. Later, in the face of barbarian onslaughts in Europe, Catholicism shaped and preserved western civilization, impacting culture, music, art, drama, literature and life. It continues to do so today.

God—Father, Son and Holy Spirit—called you into being and loves you madly. God is not just an impersonal, distant, disinterested force that leaves us to fend for ourselves; God is with us constantly. Although the Catholic Church may seem to have an abundance of rules and spiritual regulations, they are actually guidelines for abundant living. They help you align the actions you choose with the beliefs you acknowledged in your Confirmation so that you may live life in Christ.

Catholics have several distinct beliefs that form the established Catholic faith and set us apart from the rest. Some of those beliefs include:

❖ The first man and woman opposed God and consequently lost many gifts for the human race—most important, eternal life. Ignorance, moral weakness, suffering, and death became a part of our world because of this original sin.

8

- God sent his Son to become human, live among people and lead them closer to God, and then suffer and die—all to atone for original sin and all the times men and women turn their backs on God by sinning.
- Jesus was born, quite miraculously, of a virgin named Mary.
- Jesus died on a cross for our salvation, rose from the dead, and ascended into heaven—making up for all sin.
- Jesus gave us the Eucharist so he could be with us throughout time.
- Jesus empowered his Church to carry on his work under the leadership of the pope (bishop of Rome) and all bishops in communion with him.
- Jesus acts through seven sacraments to grace us at key moments of life.
- At the end of the world, Jesus will return to earth to judge all people.
- Our intended destiny is an eternal afterlife of perfect happiness with God.

Being Catholic is not easy. In the early days of the Church, Christians were tortured and killed for their beliefs. Throughout history—and even in some parts of the world today—some Catholics have been persecuted and forced to hide their faith. This happened in England when King Henry VIII declared himself leader of the Church. It has been a reality for Catholics in China for the past fifty years. Jesus, however, reminds us: "I am with you always, to the end of the age" (Matthew 28:20), encouraging generations of Christians who share in his suffering because of their faith.

When the mostly Protestant founders first formed the United States, many of them held disdain for the Catholic Church from which they had broken away. As a result of the animosity toward

fyi...

The Church has four distinct marks or characteristics. Since 381 A.D. it has been described as one, holy, catholic (universal or open to all), and apostolic (having continuity with the apostles).

big book search...

Do you wonder how Jesus established the Catholic Church? You can find the story in Matthew 16:13-20. In John 10:11-18 Jesus declared, "I am the good shepherd." You can find the story of Jesus' asking Peter to feed his sheep in John 21:15-17.

a cool
website...

The United States
Conference of
Catholic Bishops
(USCCB) produces
documents on a vari-
ety of topics. Find
more about this or-
ganization and access
its documents at
www.usccb.org. At
this site you can also
find movie reviews,
Church facts, and the
daily readings.

Rome, early American Catholics were treated with scorn and suspicion. They were excluded from the first English settlements—except for Maryland and Pennsylvania. Although the first amendment to the Constitution guaranteed religious freedom in 1789, many states upheld discriminatory laws against Catholics well into the nineteenth century. Both the Know-Nothings and the Ku Klux Klan led violence against Catholics, murdering them and burning their buildings. Not until 1963 did a Catholic—John F. Kennedy—serve as President of the United States.

Standing up for justice and life are part of our mission as Catholics. Jesus said: "I am the way and the truth and the life" (John 14:6). Accepting this mission can cause us to feel at odds with our contemporary culture. It does not mean just opposing abortion or capital punishment, but demanding a more abundant life for the poor and persecuted. We are challenged to promote lifelong fidelity at a time when divorce is rampant, and we reserve sex as an expression of total commitment and love in marriage instead of using it as meaningless recreation. Living an abundant Catholic faith means choosing peace instead of war, justice over self-interest, outreach to the poor instead of materialism, and love over hate.

Sometimes these convictions make the Catholic faith unpopular among contemporary American ideologies. The Church has also faced negative publicity due to the actions of clergy and laity alike—the failures of each of us to live as perfectly as Jesus did and to "practice what we preach" in our daily lives. However, author Brennan Manning notes that the Church is not a museum of saints—or else we would all be locked out! Rather, the Church is a hospital for sinners—a community that encourages us to experience more fully the abundant life Jesus craves for us. Many of us Catholics are proud of our faith and values—and willingly acknowledge that we don't always get it right. But we trust that Jesus is still with his Church and strive to live faithful to his teachings. We try to grow in understanding our faith … and pray for help in living it.

Who's in Charge?

Jesus is the head of the Church—referred to as the *Body of Christ* in Paul's epistles. Bishops are the leaders of that *body* and are referred to as the shepherds of the Church because they carry out Jesus' request of Peter to "feed my sheep." The pope is the visible head of the Church, holding the position of bishop of Rome. Bishops teach, govern, and lead people to holiness. They are each given a part of the flock to tend—usually a geographical area of Catholics called a see or a diocese (meaning "city of God"). The bishop is the pastor of his diocese's principal church, the cathedral (meaning "seat") and is also the CEO of the diocesan offices known as the chancery. In the United States alone, there are 195 dioceses.

The United States bishops minister to the whole country through the United States Conference of Catholic Bishops (USCCB). Twice a year all the U.S. bishops assemble to discuss issues and make decisions regarding the national Church. An ecumenical council, a meeting of all the bishops in the world, has supreme authority in the Church. There have been twenty-one ecumenical councils. The first council was the Council of Jerusalem. At this council, the apostles decided that Gentile converts would not have to follow Jewish practices.

fyi...

The last ecumenical council was the Second Vatican Council (1962 to 1965), called by Pope John XXIII to "open a window and let in fresh air." (Some say he let in a gale!) The 2,860 bishops who attended produced sixteen documents to renew the Church so that it better serves the contemporary Body of Christ.

big book search...

Read Acts of the Apostles chapter 15 to learn about the Council of Jerusalem.

quick quote...

Where Peter is, there is the Church. Where the Church is, there is Jesus Christ. Where Jesus Christ is, there is eternal salvation.

—St. Ambrose

Who is your bishop?_____

What is your diocese? _____

Who is your pastor? _____

What is your parish?_____

The pope shepherds and governs the universal Church from his home and office in Vatican City within the city of Rome. The pope's cathedral is the Basilica of St. John Lateran, though most papal ceremonies are held in the Basilica of St. Peter—the second largest church in Christendom. (The largest church is the Basilica of Our Lady Queen of Peace in Côte d'Ivoire.) From Peter to Pope Benedict XVI, there have been 265 popes since Jesus first established the Church.

Have you ever wondered what the pope does all day? He acts as the spiritual leader of the Church, preaches, celebrates Masses, and blesses pilgrims who fill Vatican Square or meets privately with groups and individuals—referred to as a papal "audience," and issues encyclicals and other documents to instruct Catholics on the teachings of the Church. In order to shepherd the Church, the pope also tends to his own spiritual life: praying, celebrating Eucharist, and receiving the sacrament of Reconciliation. In addition, the pope serves the Church in an administrative capacity, making leadership and organizational decisions related to the Church (e.g., appointing new bishops), drafting policy documents (e.g., issuing statements on liturgical practices), and meeting with bishops who must visit him every five years. Finally, the pope is a highly respected world leader, often filling a diplomatic role: addressing the United Nations and other world leaders as a fellow statesman. The Holy See has full diplomatic relations with 179 countries.

The *Roman Curia* is the Church's administrative agencies that are based at the Vatican and consist of the secretary of state and nine congregations, each dealing with a different aspect of the Church. The pope and *curia* are referred to as *the Holy See.*

The cardinals are another group "in charge" of the Church. Considered the *princes* of the Church and known collectively as the College of Cardinals, they are bishops appointed by the pope to advise him. Cardinals serve in departments of the *Roman Curia* and, until they turn eighty, have the power to vote in the election of a new pope. Today there are 214 cardinals, 125 of whom are eligible to vote for the next pope.

Much like governments have a legal code, the Church has ecclesial laws called the Code of Canon Law. Legislated by ecclesial authority, canon law gives practical directives, guiding the leaders and followers of the Church alike. The Code of Canon Law was most recently revised in 1983. One familiar use of canon law is in the annulment process— the process of declaring that a relationship lacked necessary foundations for valid marriage from the beginning. Just as judicial systems interpret laws governing the divorce process and entitlements, the Church interprets canon law in annulment proceedings.

Prayer for the Pope

Let us pray for our Most Holy Father, (insert name of
   current pope).
*May the Lord preserve him and give him life, make
   him blessed upon the earth,
and deliver him not up to the will of his enemies.
   Amen.*

DID YOU KNOW?

❖ You can write a letter to the Holy Father, using the salutation "Your Holiness." Address the letter like this:

> His Holiness
> Pope <insert name>
> Vatican City State 00120

❖ Vatican City is the smallest sovereign state in the world—108.7 acres with a population of one-thousand. It has a flag, its own stamps and coins, a daily newspaper (*L'Osservatore Romano*), and an astronomical observatory. Also, *Vatican Radio* broadcasts programs in thirty-seven languages. Vatican City is home to Vatican Museums as well as the prestigious Vatican Library—an impressive aggregate of nearly two million books that includes many rare collections. The Vatican secret archives is also in the city, containing documents dating as far back as the twelfth century.

❖ The papal flag is yellow and white and bears the papal insignia: a triple crown over two crossed keys, one gold and the other silver, tied with a red cord with two tassels. The triple crown represents the teaching, sanctifying, and ruling roles of the pope. The keys symbolize his authority.

❖ The Swiss Guard has performed services of honor and order and have been responsible for the pope's safety since 1506. When the forces of Emperor Charles V sacked Rome in 1527, nearly 150 Swiss Guard members sacrificed their lives, making it possible for the pope to escape. Vatican legend attributes the design of the colorful blue-red-and-orange-striped uniforms of the Swiss Guard to Michelangelo.

❖ Cardinals elect the pope in strict secrecy in an event called the *conclave* (meaning "with key"). After celebrating Mass, the eligible cardinals file into the Vatican's Sistine Chapel, and the conclave doors are sealed. The cardinals discuss proposed candidates and then cast private ballots on the altar of the Sistine Chapel. Two-thirds of the votes are required for a new pope to be elected. Following each discussion and vote, if a two-thirds majority is not reached, the ballots are burned with chemicals so that black smoke pours out of the Vatican chimney telling the outside world they are still without a pope. Once a new pope has been chosen, the ballots are burned without chemicals to send white smoke billowing out of the Vatican chimney.

The Parish: Where the Action Is

Your experience of the universal Church is most likely found in your parish, the local community of people led by your pastor. You celebrate the Eucharist and other sacraments with this community. Together you carry out works of mercy as directed in Matthew 5:7.

A parish is only as good as its members. One way to discover abundant living is to follow Jesus'example of service by sharing in community. In Luke 10, Jesus tells the story of the good Samaritan who saw a man stripped and beaten and left for dead. Others passed by, but the Samaritan man was moved with pity and stopped to care for the man. Jesus instructs: "Go and do likewise" (Luke 10:38). In addition, just as the early Christians—including the apostles—were encouraged in community, participating in parish life strengthens you to live your Catholic faith. Your parish has a variety of activities to introduce you to other Catholics, get involved in your faith community, and serve the larger world. Consider volunteering for the following opportunities and any others your parish offers:

Parish council—Check with your pastor to see if this is an elected or appointed position.

Choir—St. Augustine said, "Singing well is praying twice."

Musicians—Play an instrument, or volunteer to turn pages for a pianist or organist.

Lector—Read one of the readings at Mass, or lead the Prayers of the Faithful.

Altar server—Serve at Mass.

Eucharistic minister—Distribute the sacred bread and offer the cup at Mass and bring Communion to the sick and homebound.

Sacristan—Help prepare the church for Mass and worship.

The title *Pope* comes from the Greek word for "father"–*pappas*. Other titles for the head of the Church include Holy Father, His Holiness, Prince of the Apostles, Vicar of Jesus Christ, Sovereign Pontiff (meaning "bridge between heaven and earth"), and Servant of the Servants of God.

15

You can contact the Holy See at www.vatican.va. This site will take you to a wealth of information about your Church.

RCIA team—Share your faith with others interested in joining the Church.

Bible study group—Join one at your parish, or start one of your own and invite others to join.

Prayer group—Pray alongside other men and women in your parish by joining a rosary, charismatic, or other prayer group in your community.

Holy Name Society—Help encourage reverence towards the holy name of Jesus.

Altar and Rosary Society—Promote devotion to the Blessed Mother in this women's group.

Parish school—Help children and Confirmation candidates learn about and love the Catholic faith.

Youth ministry—Mentor a teen; lead a teen Bible study, retreat or music group.

Bereavement ministry—Cook a meal for a parishioner coping with loss; assist a support group leader.

Catholic Members

Catholics are everywhere! One of the fun things about being Catholic is the large community of believers who share your faith. In many parts of the United States, there is a Catholic parish in every town—in some cities, they're in every neighborhood! Many celebrities are Catholic.

SOME CATHOLIC VIPS

Liam Neeson—star of stage and screen who played in *Les Miserables* and *Schindler's List*

Martin Sheen—U.S. President in the TV show *The West Wing*

Paul Newman—actor, founder of the Paul Newman food brand who donates profits to charities

Celine Dion—singer, popular Las Vegas performer

Ben Affleck—Academy Award winning actor and co-writer of *Good Will Hunting* (1997)

Minnie Driver—actress in more than thirty films including *Circle of Friends* (1995) and *Phantom of the Opera* (2004)

Regis Philbin—host, *Live!* talk show and *Who Wants to Be a Millionaire* game show

John Cusack—actor who co-wrote and played in *Grosse Pointe Blank* (1997)

Jim Caviezel—actor in more than twenty movies including *The Passion of the Christ* (2004)

Tara Lipinski—youngest figure skater in history to win the Olympic gold medal

Mel Gibson—movie star who played in *Braveheart* and *The Patriot*, producer of *The Passion of the Christ* film

Ray Romano—television star of *Everybody Loves Raymond*

Adele—Grammy-winning pop and soul singer-songwriter from London

Aaron Neville—rhythm-and-blues artist known for secular and gospel songs

Sister Helen Prejean—Catholic religious whose story of befriending a man on death row is told in her book and the movie *Dead Man Walking*

Paul McCartney—musician in the popular band *The Beatles* who grew up in a Catholic family

Around the world, Catholics share the same core beliefs and are united under the same leadership hierarchy. Catholics, however, are a mixed bag. Blessed Teresa of Calcutta was a Catholic, so was Hitler. There are many "brands" of Catholics: those who declare they are Catholics *in name only*, *fallen-away* Catholics, *lukewarm* Catholics, *devout* Catholics, and *activist* Catholics. There are Catholics who are anxious for the Church to change and Catholics who wish things were the way they used to be before the Second Vatican Council.

What kind of Catholic are you? What kind of Catholic would you like to be? If there is a difference, remember that the choice is yours—labels are for jars, not people; you can easily redefine your commitment to Christ at any time by the power of free will. It is possible for you to be a lifelong Catholic, committed to Jesus Christ, living a life of faith and integrity, and dedicated to going forth from Mass *to love and serve the Lord.* All it takes is some effort on your part—and a healthy dose of God's grace.

Don't be surprised if at times you struggle with your faith. Even the saints had doubts and temptations. This is how spiritual life grows. Singing a song of trust, David has the voice of God say: "Be still, and know that I am God" (Psalm 46:10). Hang in there and count on God's help. Remember that faith gives meaning to your life. Without it, nothing makes sense.

Why are you glad to be a Catholic? _____
_____
_____
_____

Describe the "brand" of Catholic you'd like to be.
_____
_____
_____

Who are some Catholics you admire? _____
_____
_____

2. Classic Catholic Prayers

I magine a loving relationship in which the parties don't speak to each other or spend time together. That's ridiculous, of course! As a Catholic who loves God, you think of and interact with God frequently. That is just what prayer is: communicating, interacting or talking with God. Just as one of the most intimate human experiences is sitting lovingly with another person in a silence of understanding that is *beyond words,* the highest form of prayer is also wordless—gazing on God with love. All prayer has the same basic goal: union with God.

Some prayers that are hundreds of years old are part of our heritage. These prayers are usually memorized—making it easy for Catholics to pray together on different occasions—and express basic sentiments toward God: praise, thanksgiving, contrition, petition and love. We fall back on these classic prayers when our own words fail us. In this chapter you will find some time-honored prayers that are a cherished part of Catholic spirituality.

What was the first prayer you ever learned? _____
_____
What is your favorite prayer?_____
_____

SETTING THE STAGE

When you pray, creating the right ambience helps you step away from your daily activities, calm your mind, and open yourself to God. You might have a particular corner of your room or particular time of day you set aside specifically for prayer in order to get in the habit of praying. Also, creating an environment that feels reverent or encourages inner calm is a good way

In the fourth century, two candidates for emperor of Rome fought at the Milvian Bridge. The night before the battle, Constantine (one of the candidates) saw a cross in the sky with the words "In this sign you shall conquer." Constantine won the battle, became emperor, and made Christianity the state religion. The cross changed from a shameful Roman symbol to a positive one.

to get started. You might try a few of these ideas:

❖ Light a candle. You may even make a candle that you only light when you pray—a special *prayer candle.*

❖ Use incense.

❖ Play soft music. This may be instrumental music or a song that has meaning. (For example, sit with the song "Worlds Apart" by Jars of Clay when you feel a deep need to talk with God about your sins or shortcomings.)

❖ Focus on a crucifix or other religious image to center on Jesus or a religious theme.

❖ Pray in a special place where you feel God's presence.

❖ Use different postures: standing, kneeling, walking, sitting cross-legged, prostrating (lying face-down on the floor), lying flat on your back, sitting on a pillow, or using a prayer kneeler.

The Sign of the Cross

With this prayer, you draw over yourself the sign of execution that Jesus transformed into a sign of victory. As you pray the words, you touch your forehead, chest, left and right shoulders with your right hand. This can signify that you offer your whole self to God. The Sign of the Cross was made over you in blessing at your baptism and at your confirmation. We make it before and after prayers. We also pray the Sign of the Cross when entering and leaving church, using the holy water at the door.

In the name of the Father, and of the Son, and of the Holy Spirit. Amen.

The Lord's Prayer

"Teach us to pray," the apostles begged Jesus one day. Jesus responded by giving us The Lord's Prayer, commonly known as the *Our Father.* The *Didache*—

20

THE DESIGN OF THE SIGN

There have been many crosses designed over the centuries. Some reflect a particular meaning or historical experience; others are named for the person who was crucified on a cross in that shape. Here are some examples:

1. The **Latin Cross** or the **Tau Cross** are most probably the shape of Jesus' cross. Romans had criminals carry just the cross bar to their place of execution.
2. The **Tau Cross** is the shape of a "T."
3. The **Greek Cross** is used by the Red Cross.
4. The **Jerusalem Cross** (evangelization cross) originated with the Crusades as a protection for crusaders. It is made of four Tau crosses that meet in the center and four Greek crosses to represent the four corners of the world.
5. **St. Peter's Cross** is an upside down Latin Cross, named for St. Peter who asked to be crucified upside-down, declaring he wasn't worthy to die as Jesus did.
6. **St. Andrew's Cross** is x-shaped like the one on which St. Andrew was martyred.
7. The **Russian Orthodox Cross** has a top bar to represent the INRI sign and a lower bar for the footrest on Jesus' cross.
8. The **Calvary Cross** stands on three steps that symbolize Mount Calvary where Jesus died.
9. The **Passion Cross** ends in points like nails or swords to indicate suffering.
10. The **Papal Cross** has three crossbars which stand for the pope's tiara (triple crown) or the two men crucified with Jesus.
11. The **Patriarchal Cross** has a smaller bar for the INRI sign the Romans nailed to Jesus' cross.
12. The **Celtic Cross** of the British Isles has a circle to symbolize eternity or the unity of Christians around the cross.
13. The **Maltese Cross** was used by Spanish royal families on their coats of arms. Its eight points represent the Beatitudes.
14. The **Hope Cross** is an anchor, a symbol of the hope the cross gives us.
15. The **Budded Cross** has three knobs representing the Trinity at each end.

the earliest known Christian writing—reveals that the early Christians prayed this prayer three times a day. The *Our Father,* considered a treasure of the faith, was and is handed on to converts to the Catholic faith in a special ritual. Today, the *Our Father* with its seven petitions continues to be a core prayer of the Catholic faith. You may have prayed this prayer countless times without much thought as to what you are really asking of God. As you read each line, ask the question: What does this say about my relationship with God?

Our Father,
who art in heaven,
hallowed be thy name.
Thy kingdom come
thy will be done on earth as it is in heaven.

Give us this day our daily bread,
and forgive us our trespasses
*   as we forgive those*
*   who trespass against us.*
And lead us not into temptation,
but deliver us from evil.
Amen.

Hail Mary

The *Hail Mary* is devoted to Mary—the Mother of God. Did you know that its words are taken from the Gospels? When we pray the Hail Mary, the first sentence echoes the angel Gabriel's greeting to Mary when he announced to her that she would bear God's Son. Elizabeth, Mary's older relative and mother of John the Baptist, greeted Mary with the words of the second sentence. The Church added the name of Jesus to the prayer as well as the final sentence that petitions Mary's prayers. When we pray to Mary, we please her Son.

Hail Mary, full of grace, the Lord is with you.
Blessed are you among women and blessed is the fruit
*   of your womb, Jesus.*
Holy Mary, Mother of God, pray for us sinners now
*   and at the hour of our death.*
Amen.

Doxology

A doxology (from the Greek words for *glory* and *word*) is a prayer of praise. This lesser doxology is prayed at the end of a psalm in the Liturgy of the Hours as well as at the end of each decade of the rosary. The "greater" doxology is the Gloria of the Mass.

Traditional "Lesser" Doxology

Glory be to the Father and to the Son and to the Holy
*   Spirit.*
As it was in the beginning, is now, and ever shall be,
*   world without end.*
Amen.

The Apostles' Creed

A creed is a statement of beliefs. Since the early days of the Church, along with the Our Father, the Apostles' Creed has been handed on to converts in a special ritual. This prayer contains our basic beliefs as Catholics—the truths taught by the apostles:

I believe in God, the Father almighty,
Creator of heaven and earth,
and in Jesus Christ, his only Son, our Lord,
who was conceived by the Holy Spirit,
born of the Virgin Mary,
suffered under Pontius Pilate,
was crucified, died and was buried;
he descended into hell;
on the third day he rose again from the dead;
he ascended into heaven,

The Latin version of the Hail Mary is the text of Johann Sebastian Bach's, Charles Gounod's, and Franz Schubert's famous renditions of "Ave Maria."

23

and is seated at the right hand
of God the Father almighty;
from there he will come to judge
the living and the dead.
I believe in the Holy Spirit, the holy catholic Church,
the communion of saints, the forgiveness of sins,
the resurrection of the body, and life everlasting.
Amen.

What do you believe in? You might write your own personal creed. _____

_____

_____

_____

The Jesus Prayer

Around the fourth century, Christian hermits known as the Desert Fathers repeated the words of this prayer over and over to help them focus their minds on God on their journey to contemplation. To pray the Jesus prayer, sit quietly, breathe in deeply, and exhale slowly. After a few minutes, begin to pray the words of this prayer in your mind: breathe in on the first phrase *(Lord Jesus Christ)*, exhale on the second phrase *(Son of God)*, slowly inhale with the third phrase *(have mercy on me)*, and slowly let out your breath with the fourth phrase *(a sinner)*.

Lord Jesus Christ, Son of God, have mercy on me, a
*   sinner.*

Names and Titles for Jesus

If there were a contest to find the person with the most names, Jesus would win. Jesus was known in his community as *Yeshua bar Joseph* or *Jesus son of Joseph*. However, we know him by many titles:

24

- Christ
- Savior
- Emmanuel
- Lord
- Son of God
- Son of Man
- Messiah
- Redeemer
- King
- Master
- Lamb of God
- Prince of Peace
- Alpha and Omega
- Lion of Judah
- Son of David
- Incarnate Word

Through the Holy Spirit we are restored to paradise, led back to the kingdom of heaven, and adopted as children, given confidence to call God "Father" and to share in Christ's grace, called children of light and given a share in eternal glory.

—St. Basil

In John's gospel, Jesus identified himself by saying, "I am," and finishing with these names:
- *the living bread* (6:35)
- *the light of the world* (8:12)
- *the gate for the sheep* (10:7)
- *the good shepherd* (10:11)
- *the resurrection and the life* (11:25)
- *the way, the truth, and the life* (14:6)
- *the true vine* (15:1)

When Jesus claimed, "I am," he identified with Yahweh who revealed himself to Moses as I Am who Am. (Exodus 3:14)

What is your favorite name for Jesus? _____

_____

What does this name mean?_____

_____

Why do you identify with this name for him?_____

_____

What name would you like him to call you? _____

_____

Come, Holy Spirit

Byzantine Catholics belong to one of the Eastern Rite churches. These churches are Catholic (in union with Rome) but developed liturgies and spiritualities based on certain cultures. They include: Coptic, Ethiopian, Chaldean, Melkite, Maronite, Syrian and Armenian. Except for the Maronite rite, all of these have Orthodox (non-Catholic) counterparts. Most Catholics of the Western Rite are called *Roman* or *Latin Rite Catholics.*

The Third Person of the Triune God, the Holy Spirit, was promised by Jesus and sent on a mission by the Father to help us live a holy life. Other names for the Holy Spirit are the Holy Ghost, Spirit of Truth, Spirit of God, Spirit of Love, Advocate, and the Paraclete. The Holy Spirit dwells within us and acts as our constant coach and inspirer. Ironically, this all-powerful friend is too often the forgotten person of the Trinity.

Come, Holy Spirit, fill the hearts of your faithful
and enkindle in them the fire of your love.
Send forth your Spirit and they will be created
and you shall renew the face of the earth.
O God, who instructed the hearts of the faithful
by the light of the Holy Spirit,
grant us by the same Holy Spirit
a love and relish of what is right and just
and a constant enjoyment of his comfort,
through Christ our Lord. Amen.

When have you felt the Holy Spirit's presence in your life? _____

_____

How might you invoke the Holy Spirit as you strive for more abundant living? _____

_____

Acts of Faith, Hope, and Charity (Love)

Faith, hope and charity are the virtues on which our relationship with God is built. They are virtues of abundant living. In 1 Corinthians 13, Paul writes about them: "And now faith, hope, and love abide, these three; and the greatest of these is love." John gives us a central Christian definition in 1 John 4:

"God is love." By praying the acts of faith, hope and love, you can grow in these theological virtues.

big book search...

Look up the prayer of praise John heard in his vision of heaven: Revelation 5:11–14. (Note: The Lamb is Jesus.)

Act of Faith
O my God, I firmly believe that you are one God in three divine Persons: Father, Son, and Holy Spirit; I believe that your divine Son became man and died for our sins, and that he will come to judge the living and the dead. I believe these and all the truths which the Holy Catholic Church teaches, because you revealed them, who can neither deceive nor be deceived.

Act of Hope
O my God, relying on your infinite goodness and promises, I hope to obtain pardon of my sins, the help of your grace, and life everlasting, through the merits of Jesus Christ, my Lord and Redeemer.

Act of Love
O my God, I love you above all things, with my whole heart and soul, because you are all good and worthy of all my love. I love my neighbor as myself for the love of you. I forgive all who have injured me and I ask pardon of all whom I have injured.

Acts of Contrition
The word *contrition* means "sincere remorse" or "repentance." Acts of contrition are prayers of repentance to God, acknowledging wrongdoings and asking forgiveness. In itself, outside of the sacrament of Reconciliation this prayer gains forgiveness for sins. It is a good practice to end each day by recalling any sins or faults committed that day and then praying an act of contrition. As a final repentance, it is also a good prayer to pray if you are in danger of death.

a cool website...

To check out Catholic news visit www.catholiconline.com.

trivial tidbit...

The Day of the Dead is a Mexican tradition celebrated on November 2, the Feast of All Souls, each year. Candy skulls, masks, puppets, and a party-like atmosphere are customary parts of the celebration, keeping with our belief that death is a doorway to new life. The celebration may also include cleaning the graves of relatives and then having a picnic in the cemetery.

Act of Contrition (traditional)

O my God, I am heartily sorry for having offended you, and I detest all my sins, because I dread the loss of heaven and the pains of hell, but most of all because they offend you, my God, who are all good and deserving of all my love. I firmly resolve, with the help of your grace, to confess my sins, to do penance and to amend my life. Amen.

Act of Contrition (short)

O my God, I am sorry for my sins because I have offended you whom I should love above all things. Help me to do penance, to do better, and to avoid anything that might lead me to sin. Amen.

For the Poor Souls

Catholics believe in praying for those who have "crossed over"—that is, the deceased—based on 2 Maccabees 12:39-46. All Church members (saints, poor souls, and those on Earth) are united in the *communion of saints* and help one another by our prayers. You might make it a habit whenever you pass a cemetery to pray the following prayer for the souls of those buried there:

Eternal rest grant unto them, O Lord, and let perpetual light shine upon them. May they rest in peace. Amen.

Some Famous Catholic Ancestors

J.R.R. Tolkien—author of the *Hobbit* tales, told in the *Lord of the Rings* movies

Blessed Teresa of Calcutta—a living saint in the eyes of many before her death in 1997; awarded the Nobel Peace Prize in 1979 for her work among the poor in India

Michelangelo—artist; painted the Sistine Chapel in Rome and sculpted many famous statues including the David, the Pietà and Moses

Bob Hope—a legendary American comedian, star of many films and television specials; famous for entertaining American troops abroad

Ludwig van Beethoven—a German musician and composer of nine great symphonies and many other classical masterpieces

Wolfgang Amadeus Mozart—child prodigy and a prolific Austrian composer who wrote more than 600 pieces of music including several world-renowned operas: *The Marriage of Figaro, The Magic Flute,* and *Don Giovanni*

Dante Alighieri—poet, author of *The Divine Comedy*

Louis Pasteur—scientist; discovered how to pasteurize milk

Graham Greene—novelist and playwright

Babe Ruth—legendary baseball player known as the *Sultan of Swat*

Nicholas Copernicus—first to propose that the planets circled the sun

John Wayne—actor; famous for Western movies (converted on his deathbed)

Vasco de Gama—first explorer to sail around Africa

Alfred Hitchcock—British film director of unforgettable, suspenseful films such as *Rear Window, Psycho,* and *Dial M for Murder*

René Descartes—seventeenth century French philosopher, mathematician and scientist

Ferdinand Magellan—first person to sail around the world

Gregor Mendel—Austrian scientist hailed as the *father of modern genetics;* an Augustinian monk

Christopher Columbus—European discoverer of the new world (the present-day Americas)

one worders...

Alleluia. The prayer *Alleluia* means "Praise God." *Hallel* is Hebrew for "praise," and *Yah* is the first syllable in the name *Yahweh*, which means "Lord" or "God."

Amen. The prayer *Amen* means "Yes, I agree."

Maranatha. This last word in the Bible means "Come, Lord Jesus."

Help. No explanation necessary!

Jesus, I believe, I adore, I hope, and I love you. I ask pardon for those who do not believe, do not adore, do not hope, and do not love you.

Flannery O'Connor—American author of short stories

Gregory Peck—movie star best known for his role in *To Kill a Mockingbird*

Leonardo de Vinci—great painter, scientist, and inventor during the Italian Renaissance

Christa McAuliffe—teacher, astronaut on the fatal *Challenger* mission

Galileo Galilei—Italian astronomer, mathematician, and inventor of the telescope

Dorothy Day—peace and justice activist who founded the Catholic Worker movement

Thomas Wyatt Turner—founding member of the NAACP and the first African-American to receive a doctorate from Cornell University

Mother Jones—American labor movement organizer

Te Deum

You've probably sung "Holy God, We Praise Your Name" at church on special occasions. It is based on a German translation of the Te Deum, a majestic hymn attributed to St. Ambrose, who lived in the fourth century. The name *Te Deum* is Latin for the first words, "you God."

You are God: we praise you;
You are the Lord: we acclaim you;
You are the eternal Father:
All creation worships you.
To you all angels, all the powers of heaven,
Cherubim and Seraphim, sing in endless praise:
Holy, holy, holy Lord, God of power and might,
heaven and earth are full of your glory.
The glorious company of apostles praise you.
The noble fellowship of prophets praise you.
The white-robed army of martyrs praise you.
Throughout the world the holy Church acclaims you:

Father, of majesty unbounded,
your true and only Son, worthy of all worship,
and the Holy Spirit, advocate and guide.
You, Christ, are the king of glory,
the eternal Son of the Father.
When you became man to set us free
you did not spurn the Virgin's womb.
You overcame the sting of death,
and opened the kingdom of heaven to all believers.
You are seated at God's right hand in glory.
We believe that you will come, and be our judge.
Come then, Lord, and help your people,
bought with the price of your own blood,
and bring us with your saints
to glory everlasting.

Save your people, Lord, and bless your inheritance.
Govern and uphold them now and always.
Day by day we bless you.
We praise your name for ever.
Keep us today, Lord, from all sin.
Have mercy on us, Lord, have mercy.
Lord, show us your love and mercy;
for we put our trust in you.
In you, Lord, is our hope:
and we shall never hope in vain.

3. Talking to God's Mother

A priest once explained the Immaculate Conception to children this way: We offer gifts not in a brown bag but gift-wrapped with lovely paper and ribbon. At Christmas, God gave us the best gift—Jesus. To present his gift of love, God used the most beautiful, most precious gift-wrap there was—Mary!

Many people—Catholics and non-Catholics alike—misunderstand the Catholic devotion to Mary. Catholics are accused of *worshiping* Mary, but that is not actually the case. We *adore* only God, but we *honor* Mary as God's mother and imitate her as the first disciple. Jesus is pleased when we honor his mother, as any good son would be. Mary's *yes* to God made her the new Eve, the new mother of the human race. Dying on the cross, Jesus said to John, "Behold your mother," and to Mary, "Behold your son." Since then, Catholics obeyed Jesus' words to "behold" our mother, faithfully honoring Mary and looking to her as our mother too—a natural fit, given that Jesus is our brother.

MARY'S PRIVILEGES

After creating Mary, God broke the mold. Because of her unique role as Mother of God, Mary was granted the following special graces:

* **The Immaculate Conception**—Mary's freedom from both original and personal sin from the time of her conception in St. Anne's womb;
* **The Virgin Birth**—Mary's conception of Jesus through the power of the Holy Spirit; she was always a virgin;
* **The Assumption**—Mary's body and soul taken to heaven at the end of her life.

The Memorare

The Benedictine monk St. Bernard of Clairvaux (1090–1153) is given credit for this well-loved prayer. The name *Memorare* is Latin for "Remember."

Remember, O most loving Virgin Mary, that never was it known that anyone who fled to your protection, implored your help, or sought your intercession was left unaided. Inspired with this confidence, we turn to you, O Virgins of virgins, our Mother. To you we come, before you we stand, sinful and sorrowful. O Mother of the Word Incarnate, do not despise our petitions, but in your mercy hear us and answer us. Amen.

The Angelus

The Angelus prayer in honor of the incarnation—God becoming man—was made popular in the fourteenth century. We think the Angelus has its roots during the Crusades (1096-1270). It is said that Pope Gregory IX ordered an evening bell to be rung to remind people to pray for the Crusades. (The Crusades were military expeditions to regain the Holy Land from the Muslims.) Eventually, bells were tolled at 6:00 a.m., noon, and 6:00 p.m., reminding people to pray the Angelus.

*V. The Angel of the Lord declared unto Mary.
R. And she conceived of the Holy Spirit. (Hail Mary...)
V. Behold the handmaid of the Lord.
R. Be it done unto me according to your word. (Hail Mary...)
V. And the Word was made flesh.
R. And dwelt among us. (Hail Mary...)
V. Pray for us, O Holy Mother of God.
R. That we may be made worthy of the promises of Christ.*

Pour forth, we beseech you, O Lord, your grace into our hearts; that, we to whom the Incarnation of Christ, your Son, was made known by the message of an angel, may by his passion and cross, be brought to the glory of his resurrection. Through the same Christ, our Lord. Amen.

The Regina Caeli

This exuberant prayer, which dates back to the twelfth century, is used in place of the Angelus during the Easter season.

V. Queen of heaven, rejoice, alleluia,
For Christ, your Son and Son of God,
Has risen as he said, alleluia.
Pray for us to God, alleluia.

V. Rejoice and be glad, O Virgin Mary, alleluia,
R. For the Lord has truly risen, alleluia.

Let us pray:

God of life,
you have given joy to the world
by the resurrection of your Son, Our Lord Jesus Christ.
Through the prayers of his mother, the Virgin Mary,
bring us to the happiness of eternal life.
We ask this through Christ, our Lord.

R. Amen.

Hail, Holy Queen (Salve Regina)

Originating in the eleventh century, this prayer is prayed at the end of the rosary.

Hail, Holy Queen, Mother of Mercy! Our life, our sweetness, and our hope! To you do we cry, poor banished children of Eve; to you do we send up our sighs,

a cool website...

Mary, under the title "Immaculate Conception," is patroness of the United States. The Basilica of the Immaculate Conception in Washington D.C. is the largest Catholic church in the Western Hemisphere. It contains shrines representing many nationalities. You can visit and tour the basilica at www.national-shrine.com.

mourning and weeping in this valley of tears. Turn, then, most gracious advocate, your eyes of mercy toward us; and after this our exile show unto us the blessed fruit of your womb, Jesus.
O clement, O loving, O sweet Virgin Mary.

Pray for us, O holy Mother of God,
that we may be made worthy of the promises of Christ.

Other Prayers Honoring Mary

Prayer to Mary
Loving mother of the Redeemer,
gate of heaven, star of the sea,
assist your people who have fallen yet strive to rise
*   again.*
To the wonderment of nature you bore your Creator,
yet remained a virgin after as before.
You who received Gabriel's joyful greeting,
have pity on us poor sinners.

Consecration to Mary
(In this prayer we offer ourselves to Mary and ask her protection.)
My Queen and my Mother, I give myself entirely to you; and to show my devotion to you, I consecrate to you this day my eyes, my ears, my mouth, my heart, my whole being without reserve. Wherefore, good Mother, as I am your own, keep me, guard me, as your property and possession. Amen.

Ave, Maris Stella
Hail, bright star of ocean,
God's own Mother blest,
Ever sinless Virgin,
Gate of heavenly rest.

Taking that sweet Ave
Which from Gabriel came,
Peace confirm within us,
Changing Eve's name.
Break the captive's fetters,
Light on blindness pour,
All our ills expelling,
Every bliss implore.

Show thyself our Mother;
May the Word Divine,
Born for us thy Infant,
Hear our prayers through thine.

The Magnificat

The Magnificat is Mary's hymn of praise, found in Luke 1:46–55. Mary sang this canticle at the visitation when Elizabeth greeted her as the mother of her Lord.

My soul proclaims the greatness of the Lord;
my spirit rejoices in God my Savior.
For he has looked with favor on his lowly servant.
From this day all generations shall call me blessed.
The Almighty has done great things for me,
and holy is his Name.
He has mercy on those who fear him
*   in every generation.*
He has shown the strength of his arm,
He has scattered the proud in their conceit.
He has cast down the mighty from their thrones,
and has lifted up the lowly.
He has filled the hungry with good things,
and the rich he has sent away empty.
He has come to the help of his servant Israel
for he has remembered his promise of mercy,
the promise he made to our fathers,
to Abraham and his children forever. Amen.

quick quote...

The knot tied by Eve's disobedience was untied by the obedience of Mary.

—St. Irenaeus

37

Prayer of St. Ephrem the Syrian

Ephrem's writing was so elegant that he received the title "harp of the Holy Spirit." His teaching about Mary won him another title, "Marian Doctor." A *Doctor of the Church* is a holy person who made great theological contributions to the Church especially through writings.

Most Holy Lady, Mother of God,
you are the only one completely pure in soul and body,
and you surpass all purity, all virginity,
    and all chastity.

You are the sole dwelling place of all the grace
    of the Spirit,
and you far surpass the Angels in purity
and in holiness of soul and body.

Turn your eyes toward me.
I am sinful and impure
and stained in soul as well as in body
with the passions and pleasures
that constitute the weeds of my life.

Set my spirit free from its passions.
Sanctify and restrain my thoughts
when they race toward adventurism.
Regulate and divert my senses.
Shake off the detestable and infamous tyranny
of my impure inclinations and passions.
Destroy in me the empire of sin.

Grant wisdom and counsel to my spirit
that is filled with darkness and wretchedness.
Help me to correct my faults and my failings.
Then, set free from the night of sin,
may I be worthy to glorify and exalt you
without reserve,

O sole true Mother of the true light,
Christ our God.

Alone with him and through him
you are blessed and glorified
by every visible and invisible creature
now and forever.

Litany of the Blessed Virgin Mary
(Litany of Loreto)
A litany is a traditional prayer of titles or phrases, after which a certain response is repeated.

Lord, have mercy.
Christ, have mercy.
Lord, have mercy.
Christ, hear us.
Christ, graciously hear us.
God, the Father of heaven,
have mercy on us.
God, the Son, Redeemer of the world,
have mercy on us.
God, the Holy Spirit,
have mercy on us.
Holy Trinity, One God,
have mercy on us.

Response: pray for us.
Holy Mary,
Holy Mother of God,
Holy Virgin of virgins,
Mother of Christ,
Mother of divine grace,
Mother most pure,
Mother most chaste,
Mother inviolate,
Mother undefiled,
Mother most amiable,

big book
search...

Mary's Magnificat echoes Hannah's words when she offered her child Samuel in the temple. See 1 Samuel 2:1–10. Samuel was the answer to Hannah's desperate prayers for a child. He became a great prophet.

Our Lady, queen of peace, pray for us!

Mother most admirable,
Mother of good counsel,
Mother of our Creator,
Mother of our Savior,
Virgin most prudent,
Virgin most venerable,
Virgin most renowned,
Virgin most powerful,
Virgin most merciful,
Virgin most faithful,
Mirror of justice,
Seat of wisdom,
Cause of our joy,
Spiritual vessel,
Vessel of honor,
Singular vessel of devotion,
Mystical rose,
Tower of David,
Tower of ivory,
House of gold,
Ark of the covenant,
Gate of heaven,
Morning star,
Health of the sick,
Refuge of sinners,
Comforter of the afflicted,
Help of Christians,
Queen of angels,
Queen of patriarchs,
Queen of prophets,
Queen of apostles,
Queen of martyrs,
Queen of confessors,
Queen of virgins,
Queen of all saints,
Queen conceived without original sin,
Queen assumed into heaven,

Queen of the most holy Rosary,
Queen of peace.

Lamb of God, who take away the sins of the world,
Spare us, O Lord.
Lamb of God, who take away the sins of the world,
Graciously hear us, O Lord.
Lamb of God, who take away the sins of the world.
Have mercy on us.

V. *Pray for us, O holy Mother of God,*
R. *That we may be made worthy of the promises of*
   Christ.

Grant, we beg you, O Lord God, that we your servants
may enjoy lasting health of mind and body, and by the
glorious intercession of the Blessed Mary, ever Virgin,
be delivered from present sorrow and enter into the joy
of eternal happiness. Through Christ our Lord. Amen.

Litany of Mary of Nazareth
The following litany is a modern one composed by
Pax Christi, an organization that works for peace.

Glory to you, God our Creator,
Breathe into us new life, new meaning.
Glory to you, God our Savior,
Lead us into the way of peace and justice.
Glory to you, Healing Spirit,
Transform us to empower others.

Response: *Be our guide.*
Mary, wellspring of peace ...
Model of strength ...
Model of gentleness ...
Model of trust ...
Model of patience ...
Model of courage ...

Our Lady of Guadalupe is the patroness of the Americas. In the sixteenth century she appeared to Juan Diego in Mexico and asked to have a large church built there. As proof of her message, Mary directed Juan Diego where to find roses, although it was December. He picked the roses, wrapped them in his cloak, and took them to the bishop. When Juan Diego let the roses fall, a miraculous painting of Mary as a lovely Mexican girl in Aztec clothing was revealed on his cloak. The cloak is displayed in the cathedral of Our Lady of Guadalupe in Mexico. Despite a normal lifespan of twenty years, the cloak made of cactus fiber has not decayed. For more information, visit www.sancta.org.

Model of risk ...
Model of openness ...
Model of perseverance ...

Response: *Lead us to life.*
Oppressed woman ...
Liberator of the oppressed ...
Marginalized woman ...
Comforter of the afflicted ...
Cause of our joy ...
Sign of contradiction ...
Breaker of bondage ...
Political refugee ...
Seeker of sanctuary ...
First disciple ...
Sharer in Christ's passion ...
Seeker of God's will ...
Witness to Christ's resurrection ...

Response: *Empower us.*
Woman of mercy ...
Woman of faith ...
Woman of contemplation ...
Woman of vision ...
Woman of wisdom and understanding ...
Woman of grace and truth ...
Woman, pregnant with hope ...
Woman, centered in God ...
Participant in Christ's passion ...
Witness of Christ's resurrection ...
Sharer in Christ's ministry ...
First disciple of Jesus ...

Response: *Pray for us.*
Mother of the Liberator ...
Mother of the homeless ...
Mother of the dying ...
Mother of the nonviolent ...
Widowed mother ...
Unwed mother ...

Mother of a political prisoner ...
Mother of the condemned ...
Mother of the executed criminal ...

Mary, Queen of Peace, we entrust our lives to you.
Shelter us from war, hatred and oppression. Teach us
to live in peace, to educate ourselves for peace. Inspire
us to act justly, to revere all God has made. Root love
firmly in our hearts and in our world. Amen.

Prayer to Our Lady of Guadalupe
Our Lady of Guadalupe, Mystical Rose, intercede for
holy Church, protect the Holy Father, help all those
who invoke you in their necessities. Since you are the
ever Virgin Mary and Mother of the true God, obtain
for us from your most holy Son the grace of keeping our
faith, of sure hope in the midst of the bitterness of life,
as well as an ardent love and the precious gift of final
perseverance. Amen.

Prayer to Mary
(Cardinal Merry del Val)
O Mary, my Mother,
how greatly I love thee!
And yet, how little is my love!
You teach me all that is necessary for me to know,
because you teach me what Jesus is for me
and what I ought to be for Jesus.

The Seven Sorrows
of the Blessed Virgin Mary

When Jesus as a baby was presented to God in the
temple, the prophet Simeon foretold that a sword
would pierce Mary's heart. This metaphor came
true by the anguish she faced in seven key events:
1. The prophecy of Simeon (Luke 2:25-35)
2. The flight to Egypt (Matthew 2:13-22)
3. The boy Jesus is lost, later discovered in the tem-

"Let not your heart be
disturbed. Do not fear
that sickness, nor any
other sickness or an-
guish. Am I not here,
who is your Mother?
Are you not under my
protection? Am I not
your health? Are you
not happily within my
fold? What else do
you wish? Do not
grieve nor be dis-
turbed by anything."
    –Mary's words to
        Juan Diego

43

---

ple—his Father's house. (Luke 2:41-52)

4. Watching Jesus carry his cross (John 19:16-25)

5. Jesus' crucifixion (Matthew 27:31-28:10; Mark 15; Luke 23:13-24:12; John 19-20)

6. Jesus is taken down from the cross. (Matthew 27:59; Mark 15:46; Luke 23:53; John 19:39)

7. Burying her son, Jesus (Matthew 27:60; Mark 15:46; Luke 23:53; John 19:41-42)

Stabat Mater Dolorosa
(attributed to Jacapone da Todi)

The hymn *Stabat Mater Dolorosa* is often sung at the Stations of the Cross and during Lent. It recalls the anguish of Mary standing beneath the cross, the pain she bore as the Mother of the Redeemer.

At the cross her station keeping,
Stood the mournful mother weeping,
Close to Jesus to the last.

Through her heart his sorrow sharing,
All his bitter anguish bearing,
Now at length the sword has passed.

O how sad and sore distressed,
Was that Mother highly blessed
Of the sole begotton Son.

Christ above in torment hangs,
She beneath beholds the pangs
Of her dying glorious Son.

Can the human heart refrain
From partaking in her pain
In that mother's pain untold?

Bruised, derided, cursed, defiled,
She beheld her tender child,
All with bloody scourges rent.

For the sins of his own nation
Saw him hang in desolation
Til his spirit forth he sent.

O thou Mother! Font of love,
Touch my spirit from above.
Make my heart with thine accord.

Make me feel as though hast felt;
Make my soul to glow and melt
With the love of Christ my Lord.

Holy Mother pierce me through,
In my hearth each wound renew
Of my Savior crucified.

Let me share with thee his pain
Who for all my sins was slain,
Who for me in torment died.

Let me mingle tears with thee,
Mourning him who mourned for me,
All the days that I may live.

By the cross with thee to stay;
There with thee to weep and pray,
All I ask of thee to give.

Virgin of all virgins best!
Listen to my fond request;
Let me share thy grief divine.

4. Universe-Wide Web: Petitioning Saints

Have you ever asked someone to "put in a good word" for you? The Church on Earth looks to the saints to intercede for us with God—to "put in a good word" when we need extra help. Saints are fellow members of the Church. They ran the race of life and attained the prize: heaven. Now they cheer us on. Most saints were ordinary people who lived extraordinary lives. They were not perfect but had "tilted halos." Although they, like us, fell into sin while on Earth, they were holy. St. Augustine was a notorious playboy before he had a conversion of heart—and life! St. Jerome had such a temper that he did not get along well with others. The saints serve as models of *imperfect* holiness for us and give us hope that while we lack perfection, we may still glorify God in all we do.

Petitioning saints means we ask them to pray for us as we grapple with living abundantly in the world. They relate to our struggles, often having faced the same challenges we do to walk the spiritual path. Just as you might ask a friend to pray for you while you're facing a difficult time, we petition the saints to pray for us. Their examples inspire us to love and serve the Lord in the midst of a broken world and temptation; their presence

---

The saint whose name we bear is called our patron saint. Who is your patron saint? _____

_____

(If you do not have a patron saint for your name, you can adopt one and ask him or her to pray for you.)

Which saint do you most look forward to talking to in heaven—and why? _____

_____

There is only one real failure in life and that is not to be a saint.

—Leon Bloy

People who are trying to sell a house sometimes turn to St. Joseph, the artisan, for help and bury a statue of him in the yard—upside down no less!

on our spiritual walk further unites us to the community of believers we were baptized into: the Body of Christ, united in glorifying God.

Prayers to St. Joseph

St. Joseph, husband of Mary and the father-figure for Jesus, is the powerful patron of the Catholic Church, of all workers, and of the dying. Although he often did not understand what God asked of him, he trustingly obeyed. St. Joseph has two feast-days: March 19 (St. Joseph, Husband of Mary) and May 1 (St. Joseph the Worker.) The month of March is dedicated to him.

Prayer to St. Joseph

O blessed Joseph, faithful guardian of my Redeemer, Jesus Christ, protector of your chaste spouse, the virgin Mother of God, I choose you this day to be my special patron and advocate, and I firmly resolve to honor you all the days of my life. Therefore I humbly beseech you to receive me as your client, to instruct me in every doubt, to comfort me in every affliction, to obtain for me and for all the knowledge and love of the Heart of Jesus, and finally to defend and protect me at the hour of my death. Amen.

Prayer to St. Joseph
(St. Pope Pius X)

O glorious St. Joseph, model of all who are devoted to labor, obtain for me the grace to work in the spirit of penance in expiation of my many sins; to work conscientiously by placing love of duty above my inclinations; to gratefully and joyously deem it an honor to employ and to develop by labor the gifts I have received from God, to work methodically, peacefully, and in moderation and patience, without ever shrinking from it through weariness or difficulty to work; above all, with purity of intention and unselfishness, having unceasingly before my eyes death and the account I have to render time lost, talents unused, good not done, and vain complacency in success, so baneful to the work of God. All for Jesus, all for Mary, all to imitate you, O Patriarch St. Joseph! This shall be my motto for life and eternity.

MORE PRAYERS TO SAINTS

Novena Prayer to St. Jude

St. Jude, glorious apostle, faithful servant and friend of Jesus, the name of the traitor has caused you to be forgotten by many. But the Church honors and invokes you universally as the patron of hopeless cases, and of things despaired of. Pray for me who am so distressed. Make use, I implore you, of that particular privilege accorded you to bring visible and speedy help where help was almost despaired of. Come to my assistance in this great need that I may receive the consolation and succor of heaven in all my necessities, tribulations and sufferings, particularly (state your request), *and that I may bless God with you and all the elect throughout eternity. St. Jude, apostle, martyr, and relative of our Lord Jesus Christ, of Mary, and of Joseph, intercede for us!*

Prayer to St. Anthony for Lost Things

Great Saint Anthony, who received from God a special power to recover lost things, help me that I may find that which I am now seeking. Obtain for me, also, an active faith, perfect docility to the inspirations of grace, disgust for the vain pleasures of the world, and an ardent desire for the imperishable goods of an everlasting happiness. Amen.

Prayer to St. Thérèse

O wondrous Saint Thérèse of the Child Jesus, who, in your brief earthly life, became a mirror of angelic puri-

fyi...

The Oratory of St. Joseph in Montreal is the main church in honor of St. Joseph. This oratory was built through the faith and efforts of St. André Bessett—a brother and a doorkeeper for his community, the Congregation of the Holy Cross. St. André had the gift of healing, and showed extraordinary devotion to St. Joseph. He raised funds for the church in an interesting way: cutting students' hair for a nickel!

49

ty, of courageous love and of wholehearted surrender to Almighty God, now that you are enjoying the reward of your virtues, turn your eyes of mercy upon us who trust in you. Obtain for us the grace to keep our hearts and minds pure and clean like yours, and to detest in all sincerity whatever might tarnish ever so slightly the luster of a virtue so sublime, a virtue that endears us to the heavenly Bridegroom. Ah, dear Saint, grant us to feel in every need the power of thy intercession; give us comfort in all the bitterness of this life and especially at its latter end, that we may be worthy to share eternal happiness with you in paradise. Amen.

FRIENDS IN HIGH PLACES

Saints are either appointed by the pope, or popularly acclaimed, as patrons for countries, people and causes. Usually a saint is associated somehow with the object of his or her patronage. For example, St. Joseph of Cupertino's gift of levitation made him a natural for patron of aviators. Here are some other saints and their causes:

Accountants – St. Matthew
Actors – St. Genesius
Artists – St. Luke
Athletes – St. Sebastian
Authors – St. Francis de Sales
Bankers – St. Matthew
Barbers and Hairdressers – St. Martin de Porres
Catechists – Sts. Charles Borromeo and Robert Bellarmine
Charitable works – St. Vincent de Paul
Construction workers – St. Thomas the Apostle
Cooks – St. Lawrence
Doctors – SS. Cosmas and Damian
Domestic workers – St. Martha
Eye diseases – St. Lucy
Farmers – St. Isidore

Foreign missions – St. Thérèse, St. Francis Xavier
Headache sufferers – St. Teresa of Avila

Canonization is the process of adding a person to the canon, or list, of official saints. The early Christians spontaneously honored the martyrs as saints. Since 1234, the pope has canonized saints after it's been proved that the person had heroic virtue or was a martyr. The local bishop gathers evidence and sends it to the Congregation for the Causes of Saints in Rome. If the cause is accepted, the Congregation appoints a relator who oversees the writing of a biography of the candidate. This account is studied by experts. With their approval, the cause goes to the pope. If he approves, the person is declared venerable. Next, if a miracle is worked through the candidate's intercession, the pope beatifies him or her, who is then called Blessed. After more study and one more miracle, the pope may declare the person a saint—a hero to be honored and imitated for his or her willingness and endeavor to emulate Christ's example. Canonization is a great celebration, usually held in St. Peter's Basilica.

Reading books on the spiritual life fosters faith. Here are some classics every Catholic should read at least once. In particular, reading biographies of the saints (or watching videos about their lives) spurs us on to imitate them and teaches us how to live our faith in the world. Visit your local library, a religious goods store, or a bookstore.

Seven Story Mountain by Thomas Merton

The Story of a Soul by St. Thérèse of Lisieux

Introduction to the Devout Life by St. Francis de Sales

Confessions by St. Augustine

Showings by Juliana of Norwich

Imitation of Christ by Thomas à Kempis

Heart patients – St. John of God
Impossible cases – St. Jude, St. Rita
Journalists – St. Francis de Sales
Lawyers – St. Thomas More
Musicians – St. Gregory the Great, St. Cecilia
Nurses – St. Agatha, St. Camillus de Lellis
Parish priests – St. John Vianney (Curé of Ars)
Police officers – St. Michael the Archangel
Postal employees – St. Gabriel the Archangel
Pregnant women – St. Gerard Majella
Schools and students – St. Thomas Aquinas
Scientists – St. Albert the Great
The sick – St. Camillus de Lellis, St. John of God
Social workers – St. Louise de Marillac
Soldiers – St. Ignatius, St. Martin of Tours

a cool
website...

The Litany of the
Saints is a prayer of
names and petitions,
asking saints to pray
for us. You can find
the litany at www.
ewtn.com/Devotion-
als/Litanies/saints.
htm.

Teachers – St. John Baptist de la Salle
Television and radio workers – St. Gabriel
Travelers – St. Christopher

Praying to Angels

Angels, too, are saints. These magnificent beings, who are pure spirits like God but created by him, praise and serve God in heaven. In Scripture there are 222 references to angels in which they often act as God's messengers, helping and protecting human beings. In the fifth century someone distinguished nine choirs or groups of angels. You are probably familiar with a few members of the archangel choir—St. Michael, St. Gabriel, and St. Raphael—from their roles in Scripture.

JUST FOR FUN

Someone made a whimsical list of patron saints by name associations. For example, the patron saint of shoppers is St. Francis de Sales. Can you guess the following patron saints?

1. Patron saint of boaters
2. Patron saint of candy makers
3. Patron saint of wimps
4. Patron saint of mortgage payers
5. Patron saint of lawyers
6. Patron saint of necklace makers
7. Patron saint of weight watchers
8. Patron saint of travel agents
9. Patron saint of pool players
10. Patron saint of sweater wearers

Answers: 1. Joan of Arc; 2. Our Lady of Mt. Carmel; 3. St. Francis of Assisi; 4. St. Bernadette; 5. Our Lady of Good Counsel; 6. St. Bede; 7. St. Josephat; 8. St. Martin of Tours; 9. St. Julie Billiart; 10. St. Casimir

Tradition holds that when some angels headed by the angel Lucifer rebelled against God, St. Michael led the good angels to victory. Lucifer and his cohorts, whom we know as Satan and other devils, were cast into hell. For this reason St. Michael is a patron of the Church. St. Gabriel was the one privileged to announce the good news to Mary that God chose her to be his Mother. St. Raphael appears in the Book of Tobit where he companions Tobit's son on a perilous journey. Not only does Jesus refer to angels in his teaching, but also they appear in his life: announcing the Good News of his birth to shepherds, comforting him in the agony in the garden, and at his tomb telling people he is risen.

A consoling teaching of the Catholic Church is that God has assigned an angel to every person to act as guide and protector on the journey to abundant life. These guardian angels watch over us to safeguard us against physical and moral evil. At one point Jesus referred to them when he said, "Do not despise one of these little ones; for I tell you in heaven their angels continually see the face of my Father in heaven" (Matthew 18:10). Many people credit their guardian angel for seemingly miraculous escapes—even for waking them up on time when their alarm clock fails to go off!

We pray *to* the angels just as we do to the other saints. We also pray *with* them: At Mass we are surrounded by these invisible hosts and join them in their continual liturgy of thanks and praise in heaven, singing, "Holy, holy, holy Lord!"

Prayer to St. Michael

Holy Michael, the Archangel, defend us in battle. Be our safeguard against the wickedness and snares of the devil. May God rebuke him, we humbly pray; and do you, O Prince of the heavenly host, by the power of God cast into hell Satan and all the evil spirits who

Do you know who the first American-born saint to be canonized was? She was a New Yorker and mother of five children: St. Elizabeth Ann Seton, canonized in 1975. St. Elizabeth's husband once helped plan a birthday gala for President Washington. After her husband died, she became a Catholic and founded the Sisters of Charity and the first Catholic school in the United States. St. Frances Xavier Cabrini was the first American citizen to be canonized (1946). Mother Cabrini, however, was born in Italy. She founded the Missionary Sisters of the Sacred Heart and died in Chicago.

Usually the Church requires that five years pass before a person's cause for sainthood is even started, and it takes years—even decades—until the process is completed. Mother Teresa was admired throughout her life for her outstanding work for the poor of India and activism through-out the world. After her death in 1997, the pope let her saint-hood review begin al-most immediately. She was beatified on Oc-tober 9, 2003—just six years after her death. Now she is called Blessed Teresa of Calcutta.

wander through the world seeking the ruin of souls. Amen.

Prayer to the Guardian Angel

Angel sent by God to guide me,
be my light and walk behind me;
be my guardian and protect me;
on the paths of life direct me.

Prayer to the Guardian Angel (traditional)

Angel of God, my guardian dear,
to whom God's love commits me here,
ever this day be at my side,
to light and to guard, to rule and to guide.
Amen.

5. Stealing Words from Holy People

Sometimes other people have expressed what is in our hearts better than we can. Have you ever heard a song on the radio that seemed to connect with what you were feeling about a person or situation? Prayers others have written may also help us connect with a season or experience in our relationship with God. Those authors give glory to God not only by their own prayer, but in their prompting another person to draw closer to the Lord. They do not mind if we use their words to pray—in fact, they are probably pleased.

Prayer of St. Francis Xavier

O God, I love you for yourself
And not that I may heaven gain.
Nor yet that they who love you not
Must suffer hell's eternal pain.
You, O my Jesus! You did me
Upon the Cross embrace.
For me did bear the nails and spear
And manifold disgrace;
And griefs and torments numberless
And sweat of agony;
E'en death itself—and all for one
Who was your enemy.
Then why, O blessed Jesus Christ,
Should I not love you well:
Not for the sake of winning heaven,

St. Francis Xavier, a close friend of St. Ignatius, was a Jesuit missionary to India, Malaysia and Japan. His dream was to go to China, but on the way there in 1552 he died. St. Francis' favorite prayer was "Give me souls."

Or of escaping hell;
Not with the hope of gaining aught,
Not seeking a reward,
But as yourself has loved me,
O ever-loving Lord.
E'en so I love you, and will love
And in your praise will sing
Solely because you are my God
And my eternal King.

Prayer of Dag Hammarskjöld

Give us a pure spirit so we can see you,
a humble spirit so we can hear you,
a loving spirit so we can serve you,
a believing spirit so we can live with you. Amen.

Prayer of St. Thomas Aquinas

Give me, O Lord, a steadfast heart, which no unworthy affection may drag downwards. Give me an unconquered heart, which no tribulation can wear out. Give me an upright heart, which no unworthy purpose may tempt aside.

Canticle of Brother Sun and Sister Moon

(St. Francis of Assisi)
Most High, all-powerful, all-good Lord,
All praise is yours, all glory, all honor
    and all blessings.
To you alone, Most High, do they belong,
and no mortal lips are worthy to pronounce
    your name.

Praised be you my Lord with all your creatures,
Especially Sir Brother Sun,
Who is the day through whom you give us light.
And he is beautiful and radiant with great splendor,
Of you Most High, he bears the likeness.

Praised be you, my Lord, through Sister Moon
    and the stars,
In the heavens you have made them bright, precious
    and fair.

Praised be you, my Lord, through Brothers Wind
    and Air,
And fair and stormy, all weather's moods,
By which you cherish all that you have made.

Praised be you my Lord through Sister Water,
So useful, humble, precious and pure.

Praised be you my Lord through Brother Fire,
Through whom you light the night
And he is beautiful and playful and robust and strong.

Praised be you my Lord through our Sister,
    Mother Earth
Who sustains and governs us,
Producing varied fruits with colored flowers and herbs.
Praise be you my Lord through those who grant pardon
For love of you and bear sickness and trial.
Blessed are those who endure in peace,
By you, Most High, they will be crowned.

Praised be you, my Lord through Sister Death,
From whom no one living can escape.
Woe to those who die in mortal sin!
Blessed are they she finds doing your will.
No second death can do them harm.
Praise and bless my Lord and give him thanks,
And serve him with great humility.

Mary Stuart's Prayer

Keep me, O God, from all pettiness; Let me be large in
thought, in word, in deed. Let me be done with fault-
finding and leave off all self-seeking. May I put away

*You make a root
below the soil flourish,
and you can make
fruitful the darkness in
which you keep me.*
                —Jean-Pierre de
                    Caussade

We can't, you must.
We're yours, lead us.
—Archbishop
Oscar Romero

Archbishop Oscar Romero of El Salvador defended his people against oppression. He was murdered in 1980 while he was presiding at Mass.

all pretense and meet others face to face without self-pity and without prejudice. May I never be hasty in judgment and always generous. Let me take time for all things, and make me grow calm, serene, and gentle. Teach me to put into action my better impulses, straightforward and unafraid. Grant that I may realize that it is the little things of life that create differences, that in the big things of life we are one.
And, O Lord God, let me not forget to be kind.

Prayer of St. John Vianney, Curé of Ars
I love you, O my God, and my only desire is to love you until the last breath of my life. I love you, O my infinitely lovable God, and I would rather die loving you, than live without loving you. I love you, Lord, and the only grace I ask is to love you eternally. My God, if my tongue cannot say in every moment that I love you, I want my heart to repeat it to you as often as I draw breath.

Prayer of St. Thomas More
Lord, grant me a holy heart
that sees always what is fine and pure
and is not frightened at the sight of sin,
but creates order wherever it goes.
Grant me a heart that knows nothing
of boredom, weeping and sighing.
Let me not be too concerned
with the bothersome thing I call myself.
Lord, give me a sense of humor
and I will find happiness in life
and profit for others.

Prayer of St. Anselm
O Lord our God, grant us grace to desire you with a whole heart, that so desiring you we may seek and find you, and so finding you may love you, and loving you may hate those sins which separate us from you, for the sake of Jesus Christ. Amen.

Prayer of St. Augustine

There are days when the burdens we carry
chafe our shoulders and wear us down;
When the road seems dreary and endless,
the skies gray with threatening;
When our lives have no music in them
and our hearts are lonely,
and our souls have lost their courage.
Flood the path with light,
we beseech thee, O Lord;
Turn our eyes
to where the heavens are full of promise!

Prayer of St. Benedict

O gracious and holy Father,
Give us wisdom to perceive you,
Intelligence to understand you,
Diligence to seek you,
Patience to wait for you,
Eyes to see you,
A heart to meditate on you,
And a life to proclaim you;
Through the power of the Spirit of Jesus Christ
   our Lord.

Mychal's Prayer

(Father Mychal Judge, OFM, was a fire department chaplain who died on September 11, 2001 at the World Trade Center.)
Lord, take me where you want me to go;
Let me meet who you want me to meet;
Tell me what you want me to say,
and keep me out of your way.

Write your own prayers in the Prayer Journal in the back of this book. Here are some ideas:

- Choose a title for Jesus (Light, Lamb of God, Good Shepherd, Savior, etc.) and write a prayer addressed to him by this title.
- Write a prayer to celebrate a feast or special occasion.
- Write a prayer of adoration, contrition or thanksgiving.
- Write a prayer about something that concerns you right now.
- Write a prayer for a certain grace you need.

O Lord, though I have no feeling of confidence in you, nevertheless, I know that you are my God, that I am all yours, and that I have no hope but in your goodness; so, I abandon myself entirely into your hands.
—St. Francis de Sales

Prayer of St. Columba of Iona

Be thou a bright flame before me,
Be thou a guiding star above me,
Be thou a smooth path below me,
Be thou a kindly shepherd behind me.
Today, tonight, and forever.

Prayer of St. Catherine of Siena

You, Eternal Trinity, are a sea so deep that the more I enter in, the more I find; and the more I find, the more I seek of you; for when the soul is satisfied in your abyss, it is not satisfied, but it ever continues to thirst for you, Eternal Trinity, desiring to behold you with the light of your light. As the hart desires the springs of living water, so does my soul desire to leave the prison of this dark body and to behold you in truth. O how long shall your face be hidden from my eyes. O abyss, O eternal Godhead, O deep sea! Clothe me with yourself, Eternal Trinity, so that I may run this mortal life with true obedience, and with the light of your most holy faith.

Prayer of St. Bernard of Clairvaux to the Sacred Heart of Jesus

How good and sweet it is, Jesus, to dwell in your heart! All my thoughts and affections will I sink in the Heart of Jesus, my Lord. I have found the Heart of my king, my brother, my friend, the Heart of my beloved Jesus. And now that I have found your Heart, which is also mine, dear Jesus I will pray to you. Grant that my prayer may reach you, may find entrance to your Heart. Draw me to yourself. O Jesus, who is infinitely above all beauty and every charm, wash me clean from my defilement; wipe out even the smallest trace of sin. If you, who are all-pure, will purify me, I will be able to make my way into your Heart and dwell there all my life long. There I will learn to know your will and find the grace to fulfill it. Amen.

Prayer of St. Elizabeth Ann Seton

Our Father, you would not willingly call on us to suffer. You say all things work together for our good if we are faithful to you. Therefore, if you ordain it: through disappointment and poverty, sickness and pain, even shame and contempt and calumny, you will support us the possession of that peace which the world can neither give nor take away.

Litany of the Love of God

(Pope Pius VI)

Lord, have mercy on us. Christ, have mercy on us.
Lord, have mercy on us. Christ, hear us.
  Christ, graciously hear us.
God, the Father of heaven, have mercy on us.
God the Son, Redeemer of the world, have mercy on us.
God, the Holy Spirit, have mercy on us.
Holy Trinity, one God, have mercy on us.
You who are Infinite Love, have mercy on us.
You who did first love me, have mercy on us.
You who commanded me to love you,
  have mercy on us.

Response: *I love you, O my God.*
With all my heart,
With all my soul,
With all my mind,
With all my strength,
Above all possessions and honors,
Above all pleasures and enjoyments,
More than myself, and everything belonging to me,
More than all my relatives and friends,
More than all men and angels,
Above all created things in heaven or on earth,
Only for yourself,
Because you are the sovereign Good,
Because you are infinitely worthy of being loved,
Because you are infinitely perfect,

a cool website...

For information about some recently proclaimed saints, go to www.vatican.va, click on the English site, then Roman Curia, Congregations, and Causes of Saints. Read about some of the saints and consider petitioning one to pray for you.

61

Pope John Paul II beatified more than 1,300 blesseds and canonized more than 480 saints, probably more than any other pope. Maybe this is because he was ordained on the Feast of All Saints!

Even had you not promised me heaven,
Even had you not menaced me with hell,
Even should you try me by want and misfortune,
In wealth and in poverty,
In prosperity and in adversity,
In health and in sickness,
In life and in death,
In time and in eternity,
In union with that love wherewith all the saints and
all the angels love you in heaven
In union with that love wherewith the Blessed Virgin
Mary loves you,
In union with that infinite love wherewith you love
yourself eternally.

Saintly Advice

❖ "Let us strive to make the present moment beautiful."—**St. John of the Cross**

❖ "Help one another with the generosity of the Lord, and despise no one. When you have an opportunity to do good, do not let it go by." —**St. Polycarp**

❖ "Love God, serve God: everything is in that." —**St. Clare of Assisi**

❖ "The gate of heaven is very low; only the humble can enter it."—**St. Elizabeth Seton**

❖ "You say you are weak? Have you fathomed the strength of God?"—**St. Madeleine Sophie Barat**

❖ "True charity consists in putting up with all one's neighbor's faults, never being surprised by his weakness, and being inspired by the least of his virtues."—**St. Thérèse of Lisieux**

- ❖ "Nothing can be more dangerous than evil companions. They communicate the infection of their vices to all who associate with them."
—St. John Baptist de la Salle

- ❖ "When an evil thought is presented to the mind, we must immediately endeavor to turn our thoughts to God, or to something which is indifferent. But the best rule is, instantly to invoke the names of Jesus and Mary, and to continue to invoke them until the temptation ceases."
—St. Alphonsus Liguori

- ❖ "Take care not to give way to drunkenness, because this sin so disgraces mankind that it lowers them beneath the unreasoning animal."
—St. Thomas Aquinas

- ❖ "Idleness begets a life of discontent. It develops self-love, which is the cause of all our miseries, and renders us unworthy to receive the favors of divine love."**—St. Ignatius Loyola**

a cool website...

For more prayers by saints go to www. catholicdoors.com.

St. Teresa's Bookmark
(found in St Teresa of Avila's prayer book)
Let nothing disturb thee,
Nothing affright thee;
All things are passing,
God never changeth!
Patient endurance
Attaineth to all things;
Who God possesseth
In nothing is wanting;
Alone God sufficeth.

6. Catholic Life 24/7

very second of our lives is a gift from God, whose constant thought of us keeps us in existence. While that sounds like a noble statement, we often forget that life is God's gift in the midst of our daily activities—waiting in line at the grocery store, sitting in traffic, working at school or at our jobs—or even when the alarm clock goes off in the morning (though perhaps sleep is the only "gift" we crave!). Our challenge is to choose abundant life—Jesus—in all that we do each day of our lives.

How do we live our faith—and live it abundantly—24 hours a day, 7 days a week? Perhaps the first step is acknowledging that we can't do it alone. Thankfully Jesus promised to be with us. To *choose* abundant life is to strive towards oneness with God. St. Paul encourages us to "pray unceasingly"—a difficult task. Does Paul mean for us to live our lives on kneelers praying the "Our Father" over and over? Our days seldom involve kneeling in quiet prayer. Perhaps Paul meant something a bit broader, encouraging us instead to live in a way that reflects God's love to the world.

Have you ever watched new parents interact with their baby? They are endeared with each new movement or coo. As the child grows older, he or she might play "mommy" or "daddy" and imitate a parent's daily work. When this happens, parents are warmed by the honor the child so innocently gives them by expressing a desire to grow closer to them by trying to do their work. Granted, a child's efforts to clean a window alongside a parent might not measure up to the parent's expertise (and may result in more smudgy fingerprints!), yet the parent is endeared by the child's attempt to emulate his or her work—and doing so the best way he or she knows. In the same way, our heavenly Father is endeared with us when we try to more closely align our lives with his—even if we smudge the window.

The key to living the Catholic faith 24/7 is being deliberate about finding God in the midst of our daily work and lives. Jesus gave us directions about how to do his work, how to imitate him: "Just as I have loved you, you should also love one another. By this everyone will know you are my disciples, if you have love for one another" (John 13:34-35).

In addition to doing God's work with love, as we strive to deepen our relationship with him, we will devote some time to focusing totally on him in prayer. This is patterned on Jesus' example. During his ministry, he prayed with his apostles and often went to pray to his Father alone. Jesus also observed the Jewish times and days for prayer, and sometimes spent whole nights in prayer. Of the twenty-four hours in our day, part of them can be spent conversing with God by following the prayer practices our Christian ancestors developed, found in this chapter.

Starting Your Day with Jesus

Awaking in the morning, it may be difficult to focus on Jesus. Any number of things may be racing through your head: all you have to do that day, all you did the day before, a struggle you're facing, the tiredness you may feel. The road to abundant life is traveled one step at a time, and starting off your day on the right foot is a great way to stay on the path. Let your first thought be one of gratitude to God for another day. You might add a simple prayer to the routine of your morning. One young Catholic begins each day with these words: "Lord, plan my day." This may sound like an overly simple prayer, but the point is not how eloquently you pray to God but rather how open you are to God's presence in your day. Becoming deliberate about focusing on God from the first minutes of your day is a helpful tool for keeping aware of the divine presence.

66

A Morning Prayer

O, Jesus, through the immaculate heart of Mary, I offer you my prayers, works, joys and sufferings of this day for all the intentions of your sacred heart, in union with the holy sacrifice of the Mass throughout the world, in reparation for my sins, for the intentions of all our associates, and in particular for the intentions of our Holy Father for this month.

Meal Prayers

As you race to the breakfast table—or grab your morning meal on the run—take this opportunity to once again express your gratitude to the Lord. Meal-time prayer is a way of thanking God for your "daily bread"—and more. During the Liturgy of the Eucharist, we are reminded of Jesus' example at the Last Supper: "He took a cup, and after giving thanks, he gave it to them" (Matthew 26:27). God is the source of all the food that nourishes us and keeps us alive. It's common courtesy to thank him.

At a missionary house in Costa Rica, a young seminarian sat down to eat his meal. He made the Sign of the Cross and immediately began eating. Others around him became agitated by his seemingly apathetic prayer, their own heads bowed much longer in prayer. After the seminarian finished his meal, he crossed himself again before leaving the table. An onlooker at another table stopped the young man as he passed by, admonishing: "Why have you ignored the Lord's blessing upon us? You don't even bother sacrificing a minute from your food to give thanks to God!" The young man replied quietly, "My friend, I apologize if my prayer offended you. My whole meal is a prayer—each bite, a new gift." He ate his meal in gratitude—a living prayer.

Praying before—or during—meals can take many forms. You may pray a traditional mealtime prayer

short prayer...

Lord, help me to remember that nothing is going to happen to me today that you and I together can't handle. Amen.

a cool website...

To find the Holy Father's intentions this month, go to www.apostlesofprayer.org.

67

God made the flowers to be beautiful, the mountains to be majestic, the animals to be diverse and to move; but God made man to serve him in the wit and tangle of his mind.

—St. Thomas More

or say one of your own. You might consider also praying for those who prepared the food or for those who do not have enough to eat.

Traditional Prayer Before Meals
Bless us, O Lord, and these your gifts, which we are about to receive from your bounty, through Christ, Our Lord. Amen.

Traditional Prayer After Meals
We give you thanks, almighty God, for all your benefits. You live and reign now and forever. Amen.

DISTRACTIONS

A man promised a friend that he would give him his horse if the friend could say the Our Father without a distraction. The friend began, "Our Father, who art in heaven." Suddenly he stopped and asked, "Do I get the saddle too?"

Prayer can seem frustrating sometimes. One moment you're listening for God's voice, the next you're making a mental list of things you have to do later in the day or thinking about the new CD you wanted to pick up. How do you stay focused? It may be reassuring to know that even the early contemplatives—those men and women who spent nearly their entire days in prayer—also struggled to stay focused. Our human minds flit about in a distracted consciousness.

Moving beyond the "noise" into the quietness where we can rest with God may seem like a daunting task. Here are tips for minimizing distraction:

❖ Sit on the edge of a chair with your spine straight.
❖ Focus on an object near you: a picture, a candle.

68

- Use a mantra, a word or phrase, to call you back to prayer.
- Incorporate your distraction into your prayer by expressing gratitude or making a plea for help.

Act of Spiritual Communion

When two lovers are separated they can call or e-mail in order to be present to each other. At times when it isn't possible to receive Jesus in Communion, you can pray the following prayer.

My Jesus, I believe that you are in the Blessed Sacrament. I love you above all things, and I long for you in my soul. Since I cannot now receive you sacramentally, come at least spiritually into my heart. As though you have already come, I embrace you and unite myself entirely to you; never permit me to be separated from you.

Work

Pope John Paul II issued an encyclical in 1981 called "On Human Work" *(Laborem Exercens)*. In it he explains the relation of work to the nature of human beings and life in society. He points out that issues of work are integrally connected with making life more human. Realistically, he shows that work can re-humanize us or dehumanize us. Sometimes this depends on what our chief goal is: to make a living or to have a life.

Many of us spend the largest portion of our day working—whether at school, home, or a job. Treating your daily work as an act of worship is therefore an important part of walking the path of abundant living 24/7. The pope uses the expression "the gospel of work." Since *gospel* means "good news," he is reminding us that work is good and, furthermore, can be used as a channel to proclaim and make God's kingdom present on Earth.

short prayer...

Jesus, for you I live.
Jesus, for you I die.
Jesus, I am yours in
life and in death!

a cool
website...

For exciting interaction, go to www.
bustedhalo.com.

Some ways of tapping the spirituality of your work include virtuous living: honesty, integrity, and consideration of others.

What are some other ways you can think of to tap the spirituality amid your daily work? _____
_____
_____
_____

What are three practical steps you can take to remind yourself that God is present and that your work is an act of worship? _____
_____
_____
_____

THOUGHTS TO GET THROUGH THE DAY

Just as God leaves his fingerprints all over our lives to remind us that he is with us, we too can encourage ourselves (and others) as we go about our day. Leaving little "love notes" of biblical wisdom or advice from saints (or others seeking God in our world) can remind us of the spirituality of our work and play. Here are some thoughts to help you as you strive to infuse your faith into your daily activities 24/7:

❖ "The same everlasting Father who cares for you today will take care of you tomorrow and every day. Either he will shield you from suffering or he will give you unfailing strength to bear it. Be at peace then and put aside all anxious thoughts and imaginations."—**St. Francis de Sales**

❖ "What is to give light must endure burning."
—**Viktor Frankl**

70

❖ "You gain strength, courage and confidence by every experience in which you really stop to look fear in the face. You must do the thing which you think you cannot do.—**Eleanor Roosevelt**

❖ "The value of our life does not depend on the place we occupy. It depends on the way we occupy that place."—**St. Thérèse of Lisieux**

❖ "Our true worth does not consist in what human beings think of us. What we really are consists in what God knows us to be."
—St. John Berchmans

❖ "Remember that nothing is small in the eyes of God. Do all that you do with love."
—St. Thérèse of Lisieux

❖ "Cheerfulness strengthens the heart and makes us persevere in a good life. Therefore the servants of God ought always to be in good spirits."
—St. Philip Neri

❖ "The best way to cheer yourself up is to try to cheer somebody else up."— **Mark Twain**

❖ "We must develop and maintain the capacity to forgive. He who is devoid of the power to forgive is devoid of the power to love. There is some good in the worst of us and some evil in the best of us. When we discover this, we are less prone to hate our enemies."—**Martin Luther King, Jr.**

❖ "No duty is more urgent than that of returning thanks."—**St. Ambrose**

❖ "When one door of happiness closes, another opens but often we look so long at the closed door that we do not see the one which has been opened for us."—**Helen Keller**

71

PRAYERS ALONG THE DAY

Prayer for Successful Work

*Direct our actions, O Lord, by your inspiration,
and further them with your continual help;
that every prayer and work of ours
may always begin from you
and through you be completed. Amen.*

Prayer Before Starting on a Journey

My holy Angel Guardian, ask the Lord to bless the journey which I undertake, that it may profit the health of my soul and body; that I may reach its end, and that, returning safe and sound, I may find my family in good health. Do thou guard, guide, and preserve us. Amen.

ODD MOMENTS PRAYER

Pray during spare time, while:

- ❖ you are on hold on the phone,
- ❖ waiting for traffic lights to turn green,
- ❖ standing in a checkout line,
- ❖ waiting for a bus or plane,
- ❖ waiting for an appointment,
- ❖ waiting for something to download.

Liturgy of the Hours: Prayer of Christians

The official prayer of the Church is the Liturgy of the Hours, prayed at seven times ("hours") of the day to sanctify the whole day. This prayer practice is primarily used by priests (it's called the "breviary") and most men and women religious, who are bound to pray it in communion with the larger Church. However, all Christians are invited and encouraged to pray the Liturgy of the Hours.

The "hours" are composed of psalms, Scripture

readings, petitions, and prayers related to the day's Mass. Typically, most people who pray the Hours (or as it is also called, the Divine Office) pray only the Morning Prayer and Evening Prayer portions. The prayers change with each day, and each liturgical season.

Night Prayer for Sunday
(from The Liturgy of the Hours, in Ordinary Time)

INTRODUCTION
God, come to my assistance.
—Lord, make haste to help me.
Glory to the Father, and to the Son,
    and to the Holy Spirit:
—as it was in the beginning, is now,
    and will be for ever. Amen.

(Brief examination of conscience, followed by the *Confiteor* on page 107 ff.)

Antiphon: *Night holds no terrors for me sleeping*
    under God's wings.

PSALMODY (Psalm 91)
You who live in the shelter of the Most High
Who abide in the shadow of the Almighty
Will say to the Lord, "My refuge and my fortress;
    my God in whom I trust!"

For he will deliver you from the
Snare of the fowler
And from the deadly pestilence;
He will cover you with his pinions,
And under his wings you will find refuge;
His faithfulness is a shield and buckler.

You will not fear the terror of the night,
Or the arrow that flies by day,

big book search...

Find Jesus' advice for praying:

Matthew 6:5–8; 7:21–23

Luke 11:5–8; 18:2–14.

John 16:23

73

a cool website...

You can find the prayers of the day at www.ebreviary.com.

Or the pestilence that stalks in darkness,
Or the destruction that wastes at noonday.

A thousand may fall at your side,
    ten thousand at your right hand,
But it will not come near you.
You will only look with your eyes
And see the punishment of the wicked.
Because you have made the Lord your refuge,
The Most High your dwelling place,
No evil shall befall you,
    no scourge come near your tent.

For he will command his angels concerning you,
To guard you in all your way.
On their hands they will bear you up,
So that you will not dash your foot against a stone.
You will tread on the lion and the adder,
The young lion and the serpent
    you will trample under foot.

Those who love me, I will deliver;
I will protect those who know my name.
When they call to me, I will answer them;
I will be with them in trouble;
I will rescue them and honor them.
With long life I will satisfy them,
And show them my salvation.

Glory to the Father, and to the Son,
    and to the Holy Spirit:
as it was in the beginning, is now, and will be for ever.
    Amen.

READING (Revelation 22:4–5)

They will see his face, and his name will be on their foreheads. And there will be no more night; they need no light of lamp or sun, for the Lord God will be their light, and they will reign for ever and ever.

RESPONSORY

Into your hands, Lord, I commend my spirit.
—Into your hands, Lord, I commend my spirit.
You have redeemed us, Lord God of truth.
—I commend my spirit.
Glory to the Father, and to the Son, and to the Holy
  Spirit.
—Into your hands, Lord, I commend my spirit.

Antiphon: *Protect us, Lord, as we stay awake; watch*
  over us as we sleep, that awake, we may keep watch
  with Christ, and asleep, rest in his peace.

GOSPEL CANTICLE (Luke 2:29–32)

Lord, now you let your servant go in peace;
your word has been fulfilled:

my own eyes have seen the salvation
which you have prepared in the sight of every people:

a light to reveal you to the nations
and the glory of your people Israel.

PRAYER

Lord, we have celebrated today
the mystery of the rising of Christ to new life.
May we now rest in your peace,
safe from all that could harm us,
and rise again refreshed and joyful,
to praise you throughout another day.
We ask this through Christ our Lord. Amen.

CONCLUSION

May the all-powerful Lord grant us a restful night
  and a peaceful death. Amen.

PRAYER TO MARY *(the Hail Mary; Hail, Holy Queen; or Regina Caeli)*

75

Ending Your Day with Jesus

Suffering out of love is better than working miracles.

—St. John of the Cross

Ending your day in spiritual reflection is a practice common among many faiths. There is something restful about reflecting on your day. American author and poet Ralph Waldo Emerson advised: "Finish each day and be done with it. You have done what you could; some blunders and absurdities have crept in; forget them as soon as you can. Tomorrow is a new day; you shall begin it serenely and with too high a spirit to be encumbered with your old nonsense." Emerson is onto something. As Catholics, we live a resurrection spirituality: each new day is a gift, each morning we are reborn into God's love and grace. Evening prayer is a chance to sit in gratitude to Jesus for walking with us that day and for the many blessings that rained down on us. We might pray the Evening Prayer or Night Prayer from the Liturgy of the Hours. In any case, end the day with an examination of conscience during the time God prepares us to rest. We resolve to live the next day as faithfully as we can, even if the present one was a failure. And that's the thing about grace: it meets us where we're at and always gives us another chance to become the best version of ourselves—God's beloved creations—on a moment's notice. All it takes is a repentant heart.

SOME NIGHTTIME PRAYERS

Evening Prayer

O my God, at the end of this day I thank you most heartily for all the graces I have received from you. I am sorry that I have not made a better use of them. I am sorry for all the sins I have committed against you. Forgive me, O my God, and graciously protect me this night. Blessed Virgin Mary, my dear heavenly mother, take me under your protection. St. Joseph, my dear

76

Guardian Angel, and all you saints of God, pray for me. Sweet Jesus, have pity on all poor sinners, and save them from hell. Have mercy on the suffering souls in purgatory (Followed by an Act of Contrition).

Watch, O Lord

(St. Augustine)
Watch, O Lord, with those who wake, or watch, or
    weep tonight,
and give your angels and saints charge over those
    who sleep.
Tend your sick ones, O Lord Christ.
Rest your weary ones.
Bless your dying ones.
Soothe your suffering ones.
Pity your afflicted ones.
Shield your joyous ones, and all for your love's sake.

Night Prayer

Lord Jesus Christ, you have given your followers an example of gentleness and humility, a task that is easy, a burden that is light. Accept the prayers and work of this day, and give us the rest that will strengthen us to render more faithful service to you who live and reign for ever and ever. Amen.

Sunday: The Pause That Refreshes

On the seventh day of creation, God rested; on our seventh day each week (on the spiritual calendar), we imitate God's example and rest. This day is called the Sabbath. Our Sabbath is the day of the resurrection and the day of Pentecost: Sunday. The Sabbath is the first of all feasts. It is also the crux of abundant living. God has more to say about the Sabbath commandment than almost any other, instructing: "Remember the Sabbath day, and keep it holy. Six days you shall labor and do all your work.

But the seventh day is a Sabbath to the Lord your God; For in six days the Lord made heaven and earth, the sea, and all that is in them, but rested the seventh day; therefore the Lord blessed the Sabbath day and consecrated it" (Exodus 20:8-11).

As Catholics, we interpret the Sabbath commandment through Jesus' example and teaching: "The Sabbath was made for humankind, and not humankind for the Sabbath; so the Son of Man is lord even of the Sabbath" (Mark 2: 27-28). In the Catholic tradition, the Sabbath is a day of joyful weekly celebration of Jesus' resurrection, something more than just a required "time out." The Sabbath is a gift from God. Often our schedules are jam-packed with places to go, people to see; the Sabbath is a little vacation, a day of refuge in the Lord, a chance to rest before diving back into the daily grind—a spiritual oasis of sorts.

We honor the Sabbath by dedicating the day to God—enjoying a day to listen to God speak in creation and to say to God, "I love you too." On this day we rest, celebrate and enjoy life—including the highest celebration, worshiping God. Traditionally, Sunday is also a day for families and communities to come together to enjoy one another and to celebrate events. It's a foretaste of heaven, the great Sabbath—eternal rest!

There are many ways of celebrating the Sabbath. Develop your own ways of enjoying the gift is a personal expression of your faith. The common thread among Catholics around the world is a Sabbath gathering for Mass. Each Saturday evening or Sunday, we gather for a Eucharistic meal, reminding us that Jesus is present in our midst. In addition, you might adopt some of these ways of resting for your Sabbath celebration:

❖ Meeting up with friends or family for breakfast after Mass

- Treating yourself to a bouquet of flowers to remind you of God's presence throughout the week
- Painting, playing music or writing—connecting with God's creative nature
- Making a holy hour of Eucharistic adoration
- Taking a walk and enjoying God's creation in nature
- Spending the day with the company of your family or community: enjoying a fun and relaxing activity, visiting elderly relatives, or enjoying a meal together
- Making time to call or write letters to friends and family you don't get to see during the week
- Simply "vegging out" while listening to Christian or spiritual music
- Reading a spiritual book in an interesting, inspiring coffee shop, park or nook

What are some things you can do to "keep the Sabbath holy?" _____

_____

_____

_____

_____

fyi...

Friday, the day of Our Lord's death, used to be a day of abstinence and parish fish fries. Today Catholics may eat meat on Friday but are still obliged to perform some type of penance that day. During Lent, Fridays traditionally are a day when Catholics pray the Stations of the Cross, remembering the path Jesus took leading up to his death and burial.

Sacrifices and Suffering

A sacrifice is a gift given to God in honor or repentance. Catholics "offer up" a variety of things: We can offer to God our whole selves, our work, as well as any hardships and suffering (crosses) we endure. Suffering becomes even more meaningful if we unite it to the suffering of Jesus on the cross—making a sacrifice of our own as we seek sanctity before God. According to St. John of the Cross, "If you do not learn to deny yourself, you can make no progress in perfection."

Penance: Spiritual Workouts

The aim of penance is to bring about a change of heart. Penance is doing difficult things such as praying when we don't feel like it or being kind to someone who drives us crazy. We perform penance to strengthen ourselves and to intentionally focus on growing closer to God.

Days of Fast and Abstinence

Abstinence and fasting are forms of penance. Abstinence in this instance refers to the practice of refraining from eating meat. Fasting is the practice of refraining from eating more than is absolutely needed, typically cutting down nourishment to one full meal and two lighter ones per day—and not eating between meals. In the United States, Ash Wednesday and Good Friday are days of fast and abstinence for Catholics between the ages of eighteen and sixty. It is also Catholic practice to abstain from meat on the other Fridays of Lent. You may not realize it, but we fast throughout the year—not just during Lent—whenever we refrain from eating or drinking an hour before receiving Holy Communion.

A GOOD FAST

Fast from discontent; feast on gratitude.
Fast from anger; feast on patience.
Fast from bitterness; feast on forgiveness.
Fast from self-concern; feast on compassion.
Fast from discouragement; feast on hope.
Fast from laziness; feast on commitment.
Fast from suspicion; feast on truth.
Fast from guilt; feast on the mercy of God.
—Author Unknown

Dedication of the Days of the Week

Traditionally, each day of the week has a specific prayer focus for the Church—in addition to the rosary mysteries and the feast of one or more saints assigned to that day. One way to connect with your Catholic heritage is by following the Church's daily dedication calendar. Perhaps you might choose a prayer for each dedication and make it part of your daily prayer routine.

Sunday	Holy Trinity
Monday	Souls in Purgatory and the Holy Spirit
Tuesday	Guardian Angels
Wednesday	St. Joseph
Thursday	Blessed Sacrament
Friday	The Precious Blood of Jesus
Saturday	Mary

short prayer...

Lord, you are like a potter, shaping us into an image of yourself. We are vessels into which you have poured life. We work with you in making the pottery of our life into something beautiful. You are worthy of all our energy and love. We want to be your disciples. This takes discipline To be a success and to make our lives beautiful by making the right and loving decisions, we need to be in touch with you. Mold us and form us so that we are not enslaved by drugs, money, power or possessions. Let us experience the real freedom to create and to love. Amen.

—Pope John Paul II

7. Christening the Whole Year

F all, winter, spring and summer: this cycle replays year after year. Corresponding to the cyclical nature of time, a rotational calendar of the Church remembers two great mysteries: the mystery of the incarnation during Advent and the Christmas season, and the great mystery of redemption during Lent and Easter.

Calendar of the Liturgical Year

❖ Advent *(beginning the Fourth Sunday before Christmas)*

❖ Christmas and the Christmas Season *(ending with the Third Sunday after Christmas)*

❖ Ordinary Time

❖ Lent, ending with Holy Week: Passion (Palm) Sunday and the Triduum (Holy Thursday, Good Friday, Holy Saturday)

❖ Easter Season *(ending with Pentecost)*

❖ Ordinary Time *(ending with the Feast of Christ the King)*

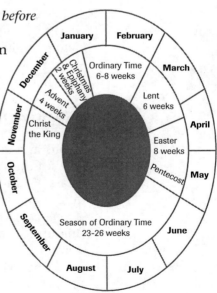

quick quote...

You also must be pre-
pared, for at an hour
you do not expect, the
Son of Man will come.
— Luke 12:40

Advent: God with Us

The month before Christmas is traditionally hectic time. Christmas cards, gifts, and parties occupy our minds and our days. It can be a draining time of year. It's hard to live the four weeks of Advent as they are intended—as a season of quiet joy and anticipation. During Advent we ponder the comings of Jesus in history (Bethlehem), in mystery (everyday in the Eucharist), and in majesty (at the end of time). We also prepare by special prayers and acts of charity to celebrate his birth on Christmas day.

Catholics have many traditions and rituals surrounding the season of Advent, intended to help prepare us for the coming of Jesus in Christmas and preserve the peaceful time of preparation, joy and anticipation. One such ritual is the Advent Wreath—an evergreen wreath with three purple candles and a pink one set around it. Each Sunday of Advent, the Church lights one candle. The pink one is lit on the Third Sunday of Advent, when we rejoice that the Lord is near. Catholics with a strong devotion to Mary may light a Mary candle daily. A white candle (representing Mary's virginity) marked with an M (for Mary), unites us with her yes to God and her time of waiting for her son to be born.

Christmas: Jesus, the Reason for the Season

Although Christmas seems to be centered on Santa Claus and gift-giving, Jesus truly is the reason for the season. The word *Christmas* literally means "the Mass of Christ," commemorating the birth of Jesus and reminding us of his ultimate sacrifice. It's easy to get caught up in the busyness of the weeks leading up to Christmas. This year try incorporating a few new traditions to help you focus on Christ, God's best gift:

❖ Bless your Christmas tree, perhaps as a family.
❖ Display a nativity scene in your home or outside.

- Sing and play Christmas carols and hymns while doing your chores or running errands.
- Send Christmas cards with a message and a stamp reminding friends and family about Jesus' birth.
- Serve the poor (wrapping gifts, serving soup, helping coordinate an adopt-a-family program or winter-coat drive).
- Attend midnight Mass on Christmas Eve.
- Make simple but thoughtful gifts for others instead of buying them.
- Pray for people who sent you Christmas cards.

Almsgiving saves one from death and expiates every sin.
—Tobit 12:9

What is your favorite Christmas custom? _____

_____

_____

Name one thing you can do this Christmas to remind yourself that Jesus is the reason for the season: _____

_____

_____

Lent: New Springtime

Like Advent, Lent is a season of preparation, but it is marked by forty days of repentance. Its hallmarks are penance, almsgiving and fasting. One of the most serious seasons of the liturgical calendar, Lent is a time of sanctifying our lives in preparation for celebrating Jesus' glorious resurrection. Catholics practice several traditions during the Lenten season.

A common question among Catholics during Lent is "what are you giving up for Lent?" Catholics sacrifice something during Lent both as a sign of repentance and as a continual reminder that it is a time of fasting in the Church. Often people give up everyday comforts, indulgences, or distractions, such as watching TV, eating chocolate, or snacking

*Christ turned all our
sunsets into sunrises.*
— St. Clement
of Alexandria

between meals. Others make a deliberate effort to give up vices such as smoking. Some more interesting things people give up are: listening to music or the radio in the car, wearing makeup, or using sugar. On the other hand, some Catholics "take up" a discipline for Lent such as daily or weekly Adoration, attending morning Mass, or even making time for daily prayer if it is not a part of their current spiritual practices. No matter what the gesture, the focus is on preparing for Jesus' death and resurrection.

There are several key days commemorating Jesus' last days before his resurrection. Holy Week begins with Passion Sunday, also known as Palm Sunday. It is celebrated the last Sunday before Easter to commemorate Jesus' entrance into Jerusalem. In Matthew and Mark's gospels, Jesus was hailed with palm leaves—a tribute used to welcome kings—as he entered the city to begin the Passover ritual.

Easter Triduum

Lent ends at the start of the Easter Triduum—Holy Thursday, Good Friday, and Holy Saturday. The Triduum, one of the holiest times of the liturgical year, lasts three days according to the Hebrew calendar: dusk to dusk. It begins with the evening Mass of the Last Supper, the main celebration of Holy Thursday—a day that commemorates Jesus' Last Supper meal shared with the apostles when Jesus washed their feet (John 13) and gave them the Eucharist (Luke 22:15, Mark 14:22-26.)

On Good Friday we remember Jesus' arrest, trial, torture, crucifixion and death. Catholics traditionally fast on Good Friday and attend an afternoon service signifying Jesus' last hours on the cross. These services may include praying the Stations of the Cross that mark the fourteen events of Jesus' suffering and death. Resurrection may be added.

The **Easter Candle** is also called the Paschal candle and the Christ candle. At the Easter Vigil the priest carves a cross and the current year into the candle and alpha and omega (Greek for A and Z) because Jesus is the beginning and the end and all time belongs to him. Next the priest puts five grains of incense in the candle for Jesus' five wounds. As the priest prepares the candle, he prays that Christ may guard us by his holy and glorious wounds. This candle stays out all during the Easter Season, and is set out for baptisms and funerals.

The pinnacle of Holy Week is at the Easter Vigil on Holy Saturday. On this day we are literally keeping watch—the meaning of vigil—as we wait for Jesus' triumph over death. At the Easter Vigil, we as a Catholic community baptize, confirm and give Eucharist to those who have been preparing to become Catholic or seek full membership—welcoming them into the Church. We also walk through our salvation history by reading from Scripture. Fire is part of the ritual, reminding us that in the darkness of death, Jesus brings the light of his resurrection. We light the new Easter candle, symbolizing a new beginning within the Church. The light from this candle is passed from person to person, each holding a taper candle, throughout the church.

Besides the many Church rituals and celebrations surrounding Lent and Holy Week, an important piece of abundant living is entering personally into the liturgical season.

The sun dance was a ritual of many Plains tribes including the Sioux. The sun dancer puts himself out for sacrifice. He is willing to offer himself, his blood, his spirit for his people. Nicolas Black Elk, a Lakota Indian who was credited with four hundred converts to Catholicism, taught that this dance foreshadows the Church's teachings about the Messiah. Jesus is the sun dancer par excellence. He offered himself as a sacrifice to save the people of the whole world.

Sometime during the year make a retreat—time carved out of your busy life to step back and tend to your spiritual life. It's a chance to evaluate your life and your relationship with God. Retreats are days of quiet and prayer, sometimes guided by a retreat or spiritual director. To find an organized retreat, check with your school, parish or diocese—as well as retreat houses and religious orders nearby. You may also make your own retreat, perhaps partaking in a weekend of silence and contemplation. Periodically you might also make a mini-retreat—called a day of recollection—to refocus your spiritual life.

What are some ways you can observe the Lenten time of repentance? _____
_____
_____
_____

Some ideas you might consider:

❖ On Ash Wednesday make a good Lenten sacrifice or resolution, a specific way to be a better Christian. Give up and/or take up something that will not only serve as a forty-day fast, but also help you remain conscious of Christ's sacrifice.

❖ Receive the sacrament of Penance. Check with your parish; often there is a Reconciliation Service for the community during Lent.

❖ Make a retreat. Whether going away to an organized retreat for a weekend or longer, or taking a day and making one of your own, make it a point to take some time to stop and reflect on the Lenten season.

❖ Participate in the rites of the Triduum. Check your parish bulletin for Holy Week calendar.

❖ Give up snacks or soda for Lent and donate the money you would have spent on those items to the poor each week.

❖ Try to replace a negative attitude you have with a positive one.

A Country Prayer for Lent

Dear Lord, we are now in the holy season of Lent. We begin to realize anew that these are the days of salvation, these are the acceptable days. We know that we are all sinners. We know that in many things we have all offended your infinite majesty. We know that sin destroys your life in us as a drought withers the leaves and chokes the life from the land, leaving an arid, dusty desert. Help us now, Lord, in our feeble attempts to make up for past sin. Bless our efforts with the rich blessing of your grace. Make us realize ever more our need of penance and of self-denial. Help us to see, in our ordinary difficulties and duties, in the trials and temptations of every day, the best opportunity of making up for past infidelities. Every day we are so often reminded in field and wood, in sky and stream, of your own boundless generosity to us. Help us to realize that you are never outdone in generosity, and that the least thing we do for you will be rewarded, full measure, pressed down, shaken together, and flowing over. Then we shall see, in our own souls, how the desert can blossom, and the dry and wasted land can bring forth the rich, useful fruit that was expected of it from the beginning. Amen.

—Author Unknown

Easter: The Mother of All Feasts

Easter is the most joyous celebration and the greatest feast of the liturgical year, commemorating Christ's resurrection and reminding us that in Christ, death is not the end but only a beginning—a new birth! At Easter we recall and celebrate Jesus Christ's triumph over sin and death; because he rose, we can hope to live forever too. Easter celebrates life, and the celebration abounds in symbols of new life in the world around us: spring flowers, butterflies, eggs and rabbits. In Lent we repented and reflected on our sins and shortcomings. In Easter we rediscover the grace that saves us that Jesus brought to us in sacrificial death and life-giving resurrection. The Church's Easter celebration reminds us to look for little resurrections in our own life as well—new beginnings, a spiritual awakening. Easter is the paradigm of abundant life.

As a Church we celebrate Jesus' resurrection by singing songs of praise and joy at Mass (including the Alleluia acclamation that lay dormant during

short prayer…

Hail Cross, our only hope!

quick quote…

Receive every day as a resurrection from death, as a new enjoyment of life; meet every rising sun with such sentiments of God's goodness, as if you had seen it, and all things, new—created upon your account and under the sense of so great a blessing.
—William Law

89

On Pentecost, Jesus
fulfilled his promise to
send his Spirit upon
them. You can find
the story in John
14:16-17.

Lent), renewing our baptismal vows, and participating in the Eucharist with renewed vigor. Churches are filled with flowers, and worshipers wear new clothes. Easter is a fresh start for everyone. Consider celebrating your gift of abundant life by doing small things to connect your personal faith with the proudest event in our salvation history:

❖ Attend the glorious Easter Vigil.
❖ Watch the sun rise Easter morning.
❖ Wear new clothes to symbolize your renewed baptism.
❖ Go for an Easter walk and observe signs of new life.
❖ Decorate Easter eggs with Christian symbols.
❖ Make a lamb cake.
❖ Gather with friends and family to share a celebratory meal after Mass.

Pentecost Sunday: Fifty Days After Easter

When the day of Pentecost had come, they were all together in one place. And suddenly from heaven there came a sound like the rush of a violent wind, and it filled the entire house where they were sitting. Divided tongues, as of fire, appeared among them, and a tongue rested on each of them. All of them were filled with the Holy Spirit and began to speak in their languages, as the Spirit gave them the ability (Acts 2:1-4).

On Pentecost, the Spirit of Jesus came upon the Church, empowering it to spread throughout the world. The Church celebrates Pentecost, the Holy Spirit's infusion into the apostles and the world, fifty days after Jesus' resurrection.

In the Church today, many Catholics maintain a strong devotion to the Spirit of Jesus. Often these men and women are referred to as charismatic Catholics, having been "baptized" in the Spirit, which involves reaffirming their commitment to Christ and inviting the Spirit into their lives. They are open to the manifestation of the Spirit's presence and gifts. Pope John Paul II, an enthusiastic supporter of the Catholic Charismatic Renewal (the organized movement of charismatic Catholics within the Church), met members in 1979 with these words of encouragement: "I am convinced that this movement is a sign of the Spirit's action, a very important component in the total renewal of the Church."

Today thousands of charismatic Catholic prayer groups meet in parishes across the globe to share in this devotion.

Veni, Creator Spiritus
Come, Holy Spirit, Creator come,
From thy bright heavenly throne!
Come, take possession of our souls,
And make them all thine own.

Thou who art called the Paraclete,
Best gift of God above,
The living spring, the living fire,
Sweet unction and true love!

Thou who art sevenfold in thy grace,
Finger of God's right hand,
His promise, teaching little ones
To speak and understand!

O guide our minds with thy blest light,
With love our hearts inflame,
And with thy strength which ne'er decays
Confirm our mortal frame.

Far from us drive our hellish foe
True peace unto us bring,
And through all perils guide us safe
Beneath thy sacred wing.

Through thee may we the Father know,
Through thee the eternal Son
And thee the Spirit of the both
Thrice-blessed three in one.

All glory to the Father be,
And to the risen Son;
The same to thee, O Paraclete,
While endless ages run. Amen.

Holy Days of Obligation

Certain days in the liturgical calendar are set aside to celebrate major events in our faith. On these days Catholics celebrate the Eucharist and avoid unnecessary work as they would on the Sabbath. In the United States there are six holy days of obligation. If the day lands on a Monday, the bishops may waive the obligation to go to Mass.

Solemnity of Mary, Mother of God – January 1
Ascension of Jesus into Heaven – Fortieth day after Easter (Thursday moved to Sunday)
Assumption of Mary into Heaven – August 15
Feast of All Saints – November 1
Immaculate Conception – December 8
Christmas – December 25

Celebrating Our Heroes:
The Sanctoral Cycle

Throughout the cycle of the church year, we also celebrate feast days of the saints and honor them at Mass. These feast days are usually the anniversary of their death—their birthday into eternal life.

Days in Honor of Mary

The Blessed Virgin Mary is one of the chief heroes of the Church because she is the mother of Jesus—God-made-flesh. It's not surprising then that Mary has several days devoted to her, commemorating significant events in her life and her major apparitions. On each feast we celebrate Mary's contribution to God's divine plan and her continued care of her children around the world.

❖ Solemnity of Mary, Mother of God – January 1
❖ Our Lady of Lourdes – February 11
❖ The Annunciation of the Lord – March 25
❖ Our Lady of Fatima – May 13
❖ The Visitation – May 31
❖ The Immaculate Heart of Mary – Saturday in June after the Feast of the Sacred Heart
❖ Our Lady of Mount Carmel – July 16
❖ Dedication of St. Mary Major – August 5
❖ The Assumption – August 15
❖ Queenship of Mary – August 22
❖ Birth of Mary – September 8
❖ Most Holy Name of Mary – September 12
❖ Our Lady of Sorrows – September 15
❖ Our Lady of the Rosary – October 7
❖ Presentation of Mary – November 1
❖ The Immaculate Conception – December 8
❖ Our Lady of Guadalupe – December 12

Dedication of the Months

Another Catholic tradition is centering devotion on a particular focus each month. It's a simple way to organize your spiritual reflection and follow the Church cycle of celebrations.

❖ January   Holy Childhood
❖ February   Holy Family
❖ March   St. Joseph

The Feast of Christ the King was created by Pope Pius XI in 1925 to give praise to Christ as supreme Lord at a time when he noticed many people's lifestyles were shifting toward increasingly worldly distractions. He recognized that the liturgy was often more effective in people's lives than proclaiming doctrine, so he used the feast day to help Catholics around the world refocus on Christ's lordship. Pope Pius XI announced the new feast saying, "Documents are often read only by a few learned people; feasts move and teach all the faithful and influence not only the mind but the heart and the person's whole nature."

- ❖ April — Holy Spirit and Holy Eucharist
- ❖ May — Mary
- ❖ June — Sacred Heart
- ❖ July — Precious Blood
- ❖ August — Blessed Sacrament
- ❖ September — The Seven Sorrows of Mary
- ❖ October — The Holy Rosary
- ❖ November — Souls in Purgatory
- ❖ December — Immaculate Conception

Feast of Christ the King

The liturgical year ends with the Feast of Christ the King, a sign that one age is ending and a new one is dawning. We await the day when Christ will come in glory to establish his kingdom of peace, justice, and love forever.

To Christ the King

(Jacques Benigne Bossuet)
King Jesus, to whom we so rightfully belong,
you have redeemed us at the cost of infinite love.
I acknowledge you as my Sovereign;
for you alone do I strive and work.
Your love will be my life,
your law the law of my heart.
I will sing your praises. I will proclaim your mercies.
I desire to be yours unreservedly.
I dedicate all my efforts to you,
to live and die in your service.

8. Making the Most of Sacraments

Jesus promised, "And behold, I am with you always" (Matthew 28:20). He keeps his promise through the seven sacraments—religious rituals of the Church, instituted by Jesus, that celebrate God's presence in our lives both on a personal level and as a community of faith. As the rites are performed, Jesus works in us to make us holy. The visible symbols within the rituals—words and signs—bring about invisible realities. Through *Baptism, Confirmation,* and *Eucharist* we are initiated into the Church; through *Reconciliation* we are forgiven; through *Matrimony* or *Holy Orders* we receive grace to carry out the vocations to marriage and ordination; through the *Anointing of the Sick* we are strengthened in sickness and prepared for death. Each major phase of life, each step in our spiritual journey holds the possibility of Jesus' help in attaining the fullness of life.

Baptism: Rebirth

Baptism is the most necessary sacrament, initiating us into the Church and permanently marking us as an heir to heaven. It is the first sacrament we receive and begins our sacramental initiation—opening the door for us to receive the other sacraments. Baptism is also the first declaration of our faith before the community. Through baptism we are reborn into Christ, cleansed of original and personal sin by water, and infused with the Holy Spirit. Whether received as a baby in a Catholic family or later as part of adult initiation into the Church, baptism joins all Christians together—practiced by Catholics, Orthodox and Protestant Christians alike.

Babies aren't the only new Catholics. The process for initiating adults into the Catholic Church is called the Rite of Christian Initiation of Adults (RCIA). Candidates go through steps marked by rituals until they are prepared to celebrate the three sacraments of initiation at the Easter Vigil service. One of the most exciting things about this process is that parish members are deeply involved in the preparation of the candidates.

HOW TO BAPTIZE

In emergency situations, anyone can baptize. Someday you might find yourself in a situation where it is necessary to baptize someone. If so, simply pour water over the person's forehead while saying the words, "I baptize you in the name of the Father, and of the Son, and of the Holy Spirit."

Renewal of Baptismal Promises

Lord Jesus Christ, I acknowledge you as king of the universe. All creation was made for you. Exercise all your sovereign rights over me. I renew my baptismal promises, renouncing Satan and all his works and empty promises, and I promise to lead a good Christian life. I will try to bring about the recognition of the truth of God and your Church. Divine Heart of Jesus, I offer all my actions that every human heart may accept your kingship. May the kingdom of your peace be established across the world, who with the same God the Father and the Holy Spirit, live and reign, God, world without end. Amen.

Reconciliation: Another Chance

The sacrament of Penance or Reconciliation is an opportunity for a spiritual makeover—sometimes an extreme makeover. Guilt and shame are ugly feelings. Sin, turning away from God through words, actions or omissions, weighs us down and cuts us off from God and others. We can be relieved of guilt and make peace through the sacrament of Reconciliation—which makes us new by grace. In this sacrament God forgives our personal sins when we confess them to a priest, are truly sorry for them, and intend not to commit them again. (The priest is bound never to reveal any sins confessed.) We have the consolation of hearing the words absolving us of our sin and receive a penance—a prayer or good work to help set us on the right track again and indicate our change of heart.

Regular repentance and reconciliation are important to abundant living. We're running a spiritual marathon—a difficult task to begin with—that becomes just a bit easier when we shed our sin and continue on our course, running to Jesus. The priest acts as our coach along the way, offering direction and encouragement—and helping untangle us from our sin—as we strive to be more loving.

Many Catholics refer to the sacrament of Reconciliation according to their role in the ritual: "Going to confession." While the priest acts as the conduit for forgiveness, our major role involves prayer, repentance, and humble confession of our shortcomings.

It is natural to be somewhat nervous about bearing your deepest secrets to someone else. Although many people prefer to sit face-to-face with the priest because it is more personal, you can also confess your sins anonymously behind a screen—especially if it will help you focus more on the sacrament's ultimate purpose: drawing you closer to God. However, if you are anxious, try talking about that with a priest. Hearing his perspective or insight may help put you at ease.

Receiving the sacrament of Reconciliation is an important part of the Catholic faith. Anytime you commit a mortal sin, first prayerfully confess it to God; and then go to confession as soon as you can. It is recommended that Catholics receive the sacrament at least twice annually, during the seasons when we aim to live our faith-life more deeply: Advent and Lent. There are three rites for celebrating the sacrament of Reconciliation:

❖ Individual confession
❖ Communal celebration with individual confession
❖ General confession and absolution (used only in exceptional cases with the bishop's permission)
(Note: In all three rites, mortal sins must always be confessed to a priest.)

Parishes offer set times for confession in a reconciliation room, usually on a weekly basis; appointments are also available upon request. Communal celebrations are often held during Advent and Lent.

How to Go to Confession: A Practical Guide

1. **Pray**. Before you even head to the confessional, pray to the Holy Spirit to help make you aware of all your sins, to be sorry for them, and to have the courage to confess them honestly. Reflect on God's love shown by his death on the cross; this will stir your heart to regret your sins.

2. **Examine your conscience**. Ask yourself these simple (yet loaded) questions: How have I failed to love God? How have I failed to love my family, friends, neighbors, strangers or enemies? How have I failed to love myself? Any serious sins will pop into your mind immediately. In addition to recalling sinful things you did, recall times you omitted doing good things when you could and should have done them. Think about the people you've interacted with since your last confession. How have you failed to love them well? Also, consider going through the commandments or the Beatitudes. There are many ways to examine your conscience. If you need help, feel free to ask a priest to walk you through it.

3. **Go to confession**. The traditional beginning to confessing your sins is "Bless me, Father, for I have sinned" but there is no set script. Something as simple as "These are my sins" will suffice. Let the priest know how long it has been since your last confession. Then begin naming any mortal sins, and if you remember, the number of times you committed the sin or any relevant circumstances. Often in the past, people recited their "laundry list" of sins. Now the Church encourages us to talk to the priest about why we sinned. This helps him guide us in avoiding it in the future.

4. **Pray**. Thank God for the grace of this sacrament and ask for help to avoid sin.

5. **Do your penance** before you forget it!

LOOKING INTO YOUR HEART
An Examination Based on the Ten Commandments
(See page 205 ff. for the Commandments that correspond to the numbers.)

Love of the Good God
1. Have you fostered a relationship with God by praying every day? Has anything taken the number one spot that God should hold in your life, such as another person, fame, money, possessions, sex or power? Have you been superstitious? Despaired of God's mercy? Have you presumed that you will be saved without any effort on your part?

2. Do you show respect for God by not taking God's holy name in vain? Have you cursed other people, spoken blasphemy, or lied under oath? Have you treated or spoken of holy things or holy people in an irreverent manner?

big book search…

In the gospels, Jesus continually showed and told how God welcomes back sinners. See for yourself by reading these passages:

Jesus' Concern for Sinners
—Matthew 9:9–13

The Prodigal Son
—Luke 15:11–32

The Pardon of the Sinful Woman
—Luke 7:36–50

The Woman Caught in Adultery—John 8:2-11

Zacchaeus, the Tax Collector—Luke 19:1–10

The Lost Sheep—Matthew 18:12–14

fyi...

To be forgiven for stealing and lying, restitution must be made. This means restoring what was taken or donating an equivalent amount to a charitable organization. For lying, reparation is making the truth known, unless to do so would hurt someone.

3. Have you always participated in Mass for every Sunday and holy day of obligation? Do you come on time and stay for the whole celebration? Have you kept Sunday as a special day of rest and relaxation?

Love of People (including yourself)

4. Have you obeyed and shown respect for your parents and for other lawful authority? Have you broken any laws? Have you been a good citizen?

5. Have you hurt anyone by fighting, mocking, unkind words, put-downs, or gossip that ruins reputations? Have you harmed, hated, or oppressed anyone? Have you sought revenge or provoked others? Have you handled anger in a positive way? Do you promote life by disapproving of abortion and euthanasia? Do you take care of your own life—avoiding drug and alcohol abuse, getting enough food, sleep and exercise? Have you given scandal or led others into sin and thereby harmed others' spiritual life? Have you forgiven anyone who hurt you? Have you asked forgiveness when you hurt another person?

6 and 9. Do you show respect for your own and others' bodies by your language, stories, and the way you dress? Do you willfully engage in impure thoughts and desires or view pornography? Do you reserve sex for use as God intended: as an expression of total love and commitment in marriage? Have you used artificial birth control? Have you broken or caused others to break marriage vows through divorce or adultery?

7 and 10. Have you damaged or stolen the possessions of others or failed to respect their right to own property? Have you returned what you borrowed?

Have you taken care of your things as well as things in public places? Have you been wasteful with God's gifts, keeping others from having their share? Have you been honest, or have you cheated someone? Have you run into debt beyond your power to repay? Have you plagiarized anything? Have you envied what others have instead of being satisfied with what you have?

8. Have you told the truth? Kept promises and secrets? Have you harmed another's reputation? Have you gossiped?

The Rite of the Sacrament

The official order of events during the sacrament of Penance is as follows:

❖ Make the Sign of the Cross with the priest.
❖ The priest or you may read from the Bible.
❖ Tell your sins. Explain why you sinned.
❖ Listen as the priest encourages you in the spiritual life. Ask any questions you may have.
❖ The priest gives you a penance (prayers or an action) as a sign that you desire to change.
❖ Pray an Act of Contrition.
❖ The priest says the words of absolution. You say, "Amen."
❖ He may say, "Give thanks to the Lord, for he is good," you respond "His mercy endures forever."

Act of Contrition (contemporary)

My God,
I am sorry for my sins with all my heart.
In choosing to do wrong
and failing to do good,
I have sinned against you
whom I should love ablove all things.
I firmly intend, with your help,
to do penance,

If we fall into sin, let us at once humble ourselves sorrowfully in his presence, and then, with an act of unbounded confidence, let us throw ourselves into the ocean of his goodness, where every failing will be cancelled and anxiety will be turned into love.
—St. Paul of the Cross

to sin no more,
and to avoid whatever leads me to sin.

Our Savior Jesus Christ
suffered and died for us.
In his name, my God, have mercy.

FORMING YOUR CONSCIENCE

Your conscience is your lifeguard, your reason telling you that something is right or wrong. Yes, we are to act according to our conscience, and we will be judged on how we follow it. This doesn't mean, however, that we can excuse our wrongdoing by saying, "But I thought it was OK." St. Ambrose warned: "Ignorance is no excuse when we have neglected to learn what we are obliged to know." We are responsible for having an informed conscience.

Here are seven ways to help your conscience get in tune with God's plan:

1. Read the Bible as well as Catholic books and magazines.
2. Talk to priests and others who are educated in theology and morality.
3. Stay close to God through prayer.
4. Make time for Christian fellowship.
5. Examine your conscience each night.
6. Celebrate the sacraments of Reconciliation and Eucharist regularly.
7. Learn what the Catholic Church teaches.

The Eucharist: Survival

The Eucharist, our highest form of worship, is a stupendous event, the source and summit of abundant Christian life. Here we encounter Christ and join in his sacrifice for our redemption, offering him to the Father and ourselves with him. In the sacrament of the Eucharist, first celebrated at our First Communion and continued as a regular part of our spiritual regimen for the rest of our lives, we give thanks to the Father (Eucharist means "thanksgiving") and are nourished with not only God's word but also the body and blood of Jesus—the word made flesh (see John 1:14). Through the Eucharist we are united with Jesus and one another as we are strengthened to carry out his mission. Moreover, our venial sins are forgiven. Celebrating the Eucharist is so essential for our abundant life that God gave us a commandment to go to Mass at least once a week; some Catholics participate in daily Mass.

big book search...

Consider praying Psalm 51, known as the *Miserere*—a prayer of repentance—before your next confession or at the end of each day after examining your conscience!

OUTLINE OF THE EUCHARIST

The Mass is a Eucharistic meal. We come together to be refreshed for our mission as Christians, to refocus on God's presence among us, to be encouraged by his word and example, and to share in the Last Supper meal Jesus celebrated with his apostles.

Introductory Rites

Greeting—The priest greets us, recalling that God is with us.

Penitential rite—We ask God to forgive our sins that separate us from him and others.

Glory to God (except for Advent and Lent)—We praise God, Most High.

Opening prayer—We pray together, silently; then the priest prays for a special grace for all of us.

Liturgy of the Word
Fed at the Table of the Word

First reading—Usually from the Old Testament, this reading is in harmony with the Gospel message.

103

Go to the holy table with your poverty and all your troubles—but also with hope and love. These are the best dispositions that you can bring to the Eucharist.

—St. Peter Eymard

Responsorial psalm—We respond to God's Word with a prayer from the book of Psalms.

Second reading—This New Testament reading is usually from an epistle. Its theme is often in harmony with the Gospel message.

Alleluia—Literally meaning "Praise the Lord," the Alleluia is our exclamation praising Jesus who will speak to us in the Gospel. We omit this prayer during Lent when we reflect on Christ's sacrifice and our own repentance, and joyfully proclaim it once again on Easter Sunday. Instead, we substitute an acclamation such as "Glory and praise to you, Lord Jesus Christ."

Gospel—This main reading of Mass, is chosen from the Gospel according to Matthew, Mark, Luke or John. In it we meet Jesus, his lessons and words.

Homily—The priest or deacon teaches us about the Gospel and readings, relating Jesus' message to our spiritual life personally and as a community.

Creed—We profess our faith by this statement of our beliefs.

Universal prayer (Prayer of the faithful)—We pray to God for the intentions of our community and world.

Liturgy of the Eucharist
The Heart of the Eucharistic Celebration
Preparation of the gifts—Community members bring up the gifts of bread and wine to offer to God (and perhaps money for the poor and for the Church). The priest prays over the gifts.

Eucharistic Prayer—This prayer of thanksgiving and sanctification is the centerpiece of the Mass when, through the Holy Spirit, the bread and wine become the body and blood of Jesus (called the mystery of *transubstantiation*), and his sacrifice on the cross is re-presented.

1. Preface—The priest praises and thanks the Father for salvation or some aspect of it.

2. Holy, Holy Lord—With angels, we praise God.

3. Eucharistic prayer—The priest asks God to bless the bread and wine, and repeats the words and action of Jesus at the Last Supper in offering the sacrifice of his body and blood *(the consecration)*. The whole Church of heaven and Earth offer Jesus to the Father with themselves.

Communion Rite—We receive Jesus under the forms of bread and wine.

1. The Lord's Prayer—We pray for "our daily bread" and for forgiveness of our sins.

2. The Sign of Peace—We extend peace to those near us.

3. The breaking of the bread—The Eucharist is broken and prepared to be shared with the community while the Lamb of God prayer is proclaimed.

4. Communion—The community shares in Jesus' body and blood.

5. Prayer after Communion—The priest prays for the effects of the mystery celebrated.

The Eucharist is not a spectator sport! Jesus invites us to fully participate in this great act of thanksgiving and offer ourselves together with him to the Father. Consider making a special intention for the Mass, singing, praying with conviction, listening during the readings to what God is saying to you and reflecting on them. Or participate in a more formal way as an usher, lector, gift bearer, Eucharistic minister, or as part of the music ministry.

Concluding Rite

Greeting and blessing—The priest says, "The Lord be with you" and blesses us.

Dismissal—We are sent out to love and serve. We thank God for everything.

Mass Lexicon

❖ Alb – white robe the priest wears
❖ Altar- table on which Mass is offered; it symbolizes Christ
❖ Ambo – the lectern, the pulpit where the readings are read
❖ Chalice – cup for the wine
❖ Chasuble – priest's vestment worn over the alb; its color matches the season of the church year or the feast
❖ Ciborium – container for the hosts, similar to a chalice with a lid
❖ Cincture – white rope the priest ties around the alb as a belt
❖ Corporal – linen square that covers the center of the altar
❖ Credence table – side table for articles used as Mass, such as the cruets
❖ Cruets – small jars for the water and wine
❖ Lavabo dish – plate for washing the priest's fingers
❖ Lectionary – book of Scripture readings for Mass
❖ Pall – linen-covered cardboard square used to cover the chalice
❖ Paten – plate for the hosts
❖ Processional cross – movable cross or crucifix that leads processions
❖ Purificator – white cloth used to dry the priest's fingers and the vessels
❖ Pyx – small container for a sacred host outside of Mass used to take Communion to the sick

- Roman Missal (Sacramentary) – book of prayers and directives for the liturgy
- Stole – long scarf worn over the chasuble

A LITURGICAL RAINBOW

During the liturgical calendar, vestments and church décor exhibit certain colors during the Mass, symbolizing different sentiments or emotions. Each color has its own meaning and season:

- Green (growth): Ordinary Time
- Violet (penance): Advent and Lent
- White (purity or glory): Funerals, Marian holy days
- Red (fire, Spirit): Pentecost Sunday, Passion Sunday, Good Friday, our Lord's passion, and feasts of apostles, evangelists and martyrs
- Black (mourning): Funerals
- Rose (joy): may be used on the Third Sunday of Advent and the Fourth Sunday of Lent

---

fyi...

The five ordinary hymns of the Eucharist—the "Kyrie Eleison" (Lord, have mercy), "Gloria" (Glory to God), "Credo" (Creed), "Sanctus" (Holy, Holy), and "Agnus Dei" (Lamb of God)—became a major musical form called a Mass. Among the many composers who produced Masses to celebrate great events are Palestrina, Monteverdi, Bach, Haydn, Mozart, Beethoven, Verdi, Stravinsky and Bernstein.

Prayer Before Mass

(St. Francis de Sales)

Divine Savior, we come to your sacred table to nourish ourselves, not with bread but with yourself, true Bread of eternal life. Help us daily to make a good and perfect meal of this divine food. Let us be continually refreshed by the perfume of your kindness and goodness. May the Holy Spirit fill us with his Love. Meanwhile, let us prepare a place for this holy food by emptying our hearts. Amen.

Confiteor

An option during the penitential rite of the Mass is the Confiteor, a prayer that emphasizes how church members are interconnected when it comes to sin and goodness:

*We can believe what
we choose. We are
answerable for what
we choose to believe.*
—John Henry Cardinal
Newman

*I confess to almighty God
and to you, my brothers and sisters,
that I have greatly sinned
in my thoughts and in my words,
in what I have done and in what I have
failed to do, through my fault, through my fault,
through my most grievous fault;*
(gently strike breast 3 times)
*therefore I ask blessed Mary ever-Virgin,
all the Angels and Saints, and you,
my brothers and sisters,
to pray for me to the Lord our God.*

Glory to God (Gloria)
This is one of the oldest Catholic hymns. It is also called the "greater" doxology.

*Glory to God in the highest,
and on earth peace to people of good will.
We praise you, we bless you, we adore you,
we glorify you, we give you thanks for your great glory,
Lord God, heavenly King, O God, almighty Father.*

*Lord Jesus Christ, Only Begotten Son,
Lord God, Lamb of God, Son of the Father,
you take away the sins of the world, have mercy on us;
you take away the sins of the world, receive our prayer;
you are seated at the right hand of the Father,
have mercy on us.*

*For you alone are the Holy One,
you alone are the Lord,
you alone are the Most High,
Jesus Christ,
with the Holy Spirit,
in the glory of God the Father. Amen.*

Nicene Creed

After centuries of heated debate and reflection, the Church set down what Catholics believe at the Council of Nicaea in 325 A.D. We still recite the Nicene Creed, the statement of faith declared at that council, today at Sunday Masses. Orthodox, Anglican, and many Protestant Churches accept it as well.

I believe in one God, the Father almighty,
maker of heaven and earth, of all things
visible and invisible.

I believe in one Lord Jesus Christ,
the Only Begotten Son of God,
born of the Father before all ages.
God from God, Light from Light,
true God from true God,
begotten, not made, consubstantial with the Father;
through him all things were made.
For us men and for our salvation
he came down from heaven,
and by the Holy Spirit was incarnate
of the Virgin Mary, and became man.

For our sake he was crucified under Pontius Pilate,
he suffered death and was buried,
and rose again on the third day
in accordance with the Scriptures.
He ascended into heaven and is seated
at the right hand of the Father.
He will come again in glory to judge
the living and the dead
and his kingdom will have no end.

I believe in the Holy Spirit, the Lord, the giver of life,
who proceeds from the Father and the Son,
who with the Father and the Son is adored and glorified,

Many Christian de-
nominations that have
Communion services
regard the bread and
wine merely as sym-
bols of Jesus. Unlike
them, the Catholic
Church believes that
Jesus is really and
truly present in the
sacred bread and
wine—body and
blood, soul and
divinity.

who has spoken through the prophets.
I believe in one, holy, catholic and apostolic Church.
I confess one baptism for the forgiveness of sins
and I look forward to the resurrection of the dead
and the life of the world to come. Amen.

Prayer Before Communion

*Father in heaven, you have made us for yourself; our
hearts are restless until they rest in you. Fulfill this
longing through Jesus, the bread of life, so that we may
witness to him who alone satisfies the hungers of the
human family. By the power of your Spirit lead us to
the heavenly table where we may feast on the vision of
your glory for ever and ever. Amen.*

Prayer Before Communion

(St. Peter Julian Eymard)
*Divine Master, Spouse of my heart, I will follow you
everywhere with Mary, my Mother. Having you, do I
not possess all riches? To love you and please you—is
not that the greatest happiness of life? To share your
sacrifices, your sufferings, your death—is not that the
most glorious victory of love? O my God, my mind is
made up! I make no more conditions or reservations in
my love for you. I will follow you in all things, yes,
even to Calvary! Speak, pierce, cut, burn! My heart is
altar and victim!*

Prayers After Holy Communion:

(Padre Pio, now canonized St. Pio)
*Stay with me, Lord, for it is necessary to have you
    present so that I do not forget you.
You know how easily I abandon you.
Stay with me, Lord, because I am weak and I need
    your strength, that I may not fall so often.
Stay with me, Lord, for you are my life and without
    you I am without fervor.
Stay with me, Lord, for you are my light and without*

you I am in darkness.

Stay with me, Lord, to show me your will.

Stay with me, Lord, so that I hear your voice and follow you.

Stay with me, Lord, for I desire to love you very much and always be in your company.

Stay with me, Lord, if you wish me to be faithful to you.

Stay with me, Lord, as poor as my soul is I want it to be a place of consolation for you, a nest of love.

Stay with me, Jesus, for it is getting late and the day is coming to a close and life passes, death, judgment and eternity approaches. It is necessary to renew my strength, so that I will not stop along the way and for that, I need you.

It is getting late and death approaches, I fear the darkness, temptations, the dryness, the cross, the sorrows.

Stay with me tonight, Jesus, in life with all its dangers, I need you.

O how I need you, my Jesus, in this night of exile!

Let me recognize you as your disciples did at the breaking of the bread, so that the Eucharistic Communion be the Light which disperses the darkness, the force which sustains me, the unique joy of my heart.

Stay with me, Lord, because at the hour of my death, I want to remain united to you, if not by Communion, at least by grace and love.

Stay with me, Lord, for it is you alone I look for, your love, your grace, your will, your heart, your Spirit, because I love you and ask no other reward but to love you more and more.

With a firm love, I will love you with all my heart while on earth and continue to love you perfectly during all eternity. Amen.

Confirmation: A Personal Pentecost

Confirmation is a sacrament that builds on the graces of baptism. It is an opportunity for a person to confirm his or her commitment to Jesus and his Church and to receive a new outpouring of the graces of the Holy Spirit.

Gifts of the Holy Spirit

If someone has a great talent, we say they are "gifted." At baptism and again at confirmation, the Holy Spirit showers us with spiritual gifts to use in the work or ministry in which we are called to serve God. The purpose of these gifts is to strengthen us for the spiritual journey ahead and to edify the Church to which you committed in the sacrament of Confirmation. The gifts of the Spirit are the traditional seven gifts listed in Isaiah 11:2–3 in a description of the savior: *wisdom, understanding, counsel* (right judgment), *fortitude* (courage), *knowledge, piety* (reverence), *fear of the Lord* (wonder and awe). The following prayer contains descriptions of the gifts as well as a request for them.

Prayer for the Gifts of the Holy Spirit
(St. Alphonsus Liguori)

Holy Spirit, divine Consoler, I adore you as my true God, with God the Father and God the Son. I adore you and unite myself to the adoration you receive from the angels and saints. I give you my heart and I offer my ardent thanksgiving for all the grace which you never cease to bestow on me.

O Giver of all supernatural gifts, who filled the soul of the Blessed Virgin Mary, Mother of God, with such immense favors, I beg you to visit me with your grace and your love and to grant me the gift of holy fear, so that it may act on me as a check to prevent me from falling

112

back into my past sins, for which I beg pardon.

Grant me the gift of piety, so that I may serve you for the future with increased fervor, follow with more promptness your holy inspirations, and observe your divine precepts with greater fidelity.

Grant me the gift of knowledge, so that I may know the things of God and, enlightened by your holy teaching, may walk, without deviation, in the path of eternal salvation.

Grant me the gift of fortitude, so that I may overcome courageously all the assaults of the devil and all the dangers of this world which threaten the salvation of my soul.

Grant me the gift of counsel, so that I may choose what is more conducive to my spiritual advancement and may discover the wiles and snares of the tempter.

Grant me the gift of understanding, so that I may apprehend the divine mysteries and by contemplation of heavenly things detach my thoughts and affections from the vain things of this miserable world.

Grant me the gift of wisdom, so that I may rightly direct all my actions, referring them to God as my last end; so that, having loved him and served him in this life, I may have the happiness of possessing him eternally in the next. Amen.

quick quote...

Make ready for the Christ, whose smile like lightning sets free the song of everlasting glory that now sleeps in your paper flesh like dynamite.
    —Thomas Merton

Fruits of the Holy Spirit

The gifts of the Holy Spirit produce qualities in us that are known as the fruits of the Holy Spirit. The Church teaches that the fruits of the Spirit are "perfections" the Holy Spirit forms in us as first fruits of eternal glory. Each fruit is a form of love.

The traditional list of the Fruits of the Spirit is based on Galatians 5:22-23. Read Paul's explanation and look for these gifts that make our lives wholesome and sweet.

❖ Charity – love
❖ Faithfulness – love proving constant
❖ Joy – love smiling
❖ Modesty – love triumphing over selfish inclinations
❖ Kindness – love showing itself sensitive to others' feelings
❖ Goodness – love making allowances and sacrifices for others
❖ Peace – love resting
❖ Patience – love waiting
❖ Continence – love exercising self-control
❖ Chastity – love respecting the gift of sex
❖ Long suffering – love enduring
❖ Mildness – love yielding

Prayer for Fruits of the Spirit
(St. Anselm)

O merciful God, fill our hearts, we pray you, with the graces of your Holy Spirit, with love, joy, peace, long-suffering, gentleness, goodness, faith, meekness, temperance. Teach us to love those who hate us; to pray for those who despitefully use us, that we may be your children, our Father, who make your sun to shine on the evil and on the good and send rain on the just and on the unjust. Grant, O merciful Father that your divine Spirit enlighten, inflame, and purify us, that he may penetrate us with his heavenly dew and make us faithful in good works; through Our Lord Jesus Christ, your Son, who with you in the unity of the same Spirit, lives and reigns for ever and ever. Amen.

Anointing of the Sick

Recent scientific research studies have found that prayer has healing power. This is no news to the Church. In James 5:14–15 we read "Are any among you sick? They should call for the elders of the church and have them pray over them, anointing them with oil in the name of the Lord. The prayer of faith will save the sick, and the Lord will raise them up, and anyone who has committed sins will be forgiven."

The sacrament of the Anointing of the Sick can be celebrated by anyone who is seriously ill, weakened by old age, or facing major surgery. Jesus strengthens and heals that person spiritually and sometimes even physically. During the sacrament, prayers are offered for the person. The priest lays his hands on the person's head and then anoints the person's forehead and hands with the oil of the sick. Communion given to a dying person after this sacrament is called *Viaticum*, which is Latin for "with you on the way." Through the Eucharist, the dying person has Jesus as a companion at the end of life's journey.

A Sick Call

If a relative is gravely ill, it is important to call the parish so that a priest may administer the sacraments of Reconciliation, Anointing of the Sick, and Eucharist. Abundant living includes abundant dying. You can help by setting a small table or stand covered with a linen cloth near the sick person before the priest arrives and placing on it: a crucifix, holy water and candles. When the priest comes into the room, if the one who is ill wants to receive the sacrament of Reconciliation, leave the room. You may return afterwards to join in the prayers. Now, the priest will celebrate the Anointing of the Sick. Finally, he will give Communion; in the case of a sick call, both the person who is ill and the caretakers may receive Communion without the usual hour of fasting.

In our Catholic faith, death is not the end but the beginning of the next life. Suffering and dying

quick quote...

Why shouldn't you believe that you will exist again after this life? Is it harder for God who made your body when it was not, to make it anew when it has been?

—St. Irenaeus

become meaningful and more bearable when they are united with Jesus' suffering and death and offered up for others.

When a Loved One Dies

When a loved one passes, it is a difficult time for all those whose lives were touched by his or her friendship and love. You may not know how to proceed at first. After a loved one passes make one of your first calls to your parish, which can be a source of strength and assistance, helping plan the funeral services including the Mass, and perhaps even providing a committee to help assist with a reception afterwards. Bereavement groups also provide spiritual and psychological support in the weeks following a death. If it is not possible for a group of people to be at a funeral Mass, memorial Masses may be celebrated for the deceased person.

If other family members are planning the funeral arrangements, you can still play an important role in helping to celebrate and bury a loved one. One of the simplest yet most loving things you can do is request a Mass be said at your parish for the repose of his or her soul. (Catholic etiquette suggests a nominal donation—between ten and twenty-five dollars—to the parish.) The day and time of the Mass, and person for whom it is being said, will be noted in the weekly church bulletin. Also, you can honor your deceased loved one by making a donation to a charitable organization in his or her name.

When a Friend (or Someone Else) Dies

Attending the wake service and funeral Mass of a deceased person is a way to celebrate his or her life and show loving support for the family. Even if you don't know what to say other than, "My sympathy on the death of your mother," your presence will speak volumes to the grieving person. It may seem like a simple gesture, but sending a sympathy card is one way to again express your condolences and show your support. It is a Catholic custom to have Masses said for a person who dies; many organizations provide lovely cards or certificates expressing this gift when a donation is made for this purpose.

Holy Orders

Holy Orders is the sacrament in which priests, deacons, and bishops are ordained to minister to God's people. Through these men, Christ teaches, guides, and sanctifies his people. Bishops, who have the fullness of orders, usually oversee a region known as a diocese and may be assisted by auxiliary bishops and a chancellor. A bishop's church, the principal church of the diocese, is known as a cathedral. When presiding at a liturgy, a bishop wears a *miter* (a pointed hat) and carries a *crosier* (a staff), symbolic of his role as shepherd of the Church.

Diocesan priests promise their bishops obedience and support them in their ministry. Priests undergo many years of training in a *seminary*, learning theology and Church doctrine and acquiring the tools and skills they will need to lead people spiritually. Since the tenth century, priests in the Roman Rite have been required to practice celibacy—giving them the freedom to devote themselves completely to Christ and his people. Priests live in a house called a *rectory* and usually serve in a parish. Some priests are given the title of *monsignor*, an honorary title.

Not all priests are diocesan priests. Some belong to religious orders or communities and take specific vows according to their order's tradition. Some orders (communities) are devoted towards a particular spirituality style, while others are focused on a particular kind of work such as missionary (service)

big book search...

Find out how the diaconate began by reading Acts of the Apostles 6:1–7.

a cool website...

Want to learn more about becoming a priest? Find out more about this vocation at www.catholicpriest.com. This website is run by the Diocese of Providence, and much of the information is specific to that diocese. However, you can also contact the office of vocations in your own diocese, or any religious order of priests.

fyi...

Permanent deacons are not to be confused with transitional deacons, men ordained as deacons as a step toward priesthood.

big book search...

Jesus worked his first miracle at a wedding in Cana at his mother's prompting. Read about it in John 2:1–12.

or monastic (prayer) orders. Many priests in religious orders serve in parishes, schools, or diocesan offices.

Deacons are another important ordained group in the Church. Their role is to assist priests and bishops and to be living signs of charity in the Church. Unlike priests, deacons may be married. The diaconate was present in the early Church and then disappeared in the fifth century. It was reestablished in 1967 after the Second Vatican Council. Now deacons can proclaim the Gospel at Mass and preach, baptize, witness marriages, preside at wakes and funerals, take Viaticum to the dying, and conduct prayer services. They do not, however, consecrate the Eucharist, hear confessions, or anoint the sick. The word *deacon* is derived from the Greek word *diakonia*, which means "service." Deacons are usually engaged in works of mercy.

Prayer for Priests

Lord, bless the priest who baptized me,
the priests who guided me in the sacrament
of penance,
the priests who celebrated the Eucharist with me,
the priests who taught me,
the priests who prayed for me,
the priests who helped me when I was in need.
Jesus, High Priest, call many more men to become
priests to minister to us and show us your face.

Marriage: Two Become One Flesh

At the wedding at Cana (See John 2:1-12), Jesus blessed the newlyweds by providing excellent wine when theirs ran out—an unfortunate event that would have branded them poor hosts and spoiled the celebration. Today Jesus continues to participate in weddings by uniting a man and woman for life in the context of the sacrament of Matrimony. Jesus teaches that in marriage the two become one flesh (Mark 10:8)—spiritually in the sacrament and literally when the marriage is consummated. With his special sacramental graces, the couple can hope to keep their vows—to show each other unconditional and exclusive love until death.

Like all the sacraments, marriage requires preparation. At least six months before their wedding, an engaged couple should contact the parish where their wedding will be held, allowing time for the Church's guidance in helping the couple know each other better and assessing their compatibility and readiness for marriage. Because, ultimately, a married couple is joined by God, discerning God's will in a relationship is an important piece of the sacramental preparation.

When you attend a wedding, what strikes you about the sacrament? _____
_____
_____

In what ways can you see God's love infusing the sacrament? _____
_____
_____

One of the ways that unity manifests itself in marriage is through the act of sexual intercourse. The Church gets a bad rap when it comes to sex. Trademark talk of chastity and the celibate culture of our priestly leaders leaves many Catholics and non-Catholics alike thinking that the Church sees sex as a bad or sinful act. Nothing could be further from the truth! Part of the reason the Church is so diligent in warning against premarital or extramar-

fyi...

A married couple, like the Trinity, is a community. Their unconditional and everlasting love is a sign of God's love. A husband and wife also are symbols of Christ and the Church, which is called the bride of Christ. Out of love, Jesus gave his life for the Church and through Communion becomes one with us. Heaven is called a wedding feast where ultimately we will be united with Christ, our bridegroom.

a cool website...

Besides Pre-Cana sessions at parishes, the Church offers retreats and programs to help couples develop happy, lasting marriages. For information go to www.engagedencounter.org.

ital sex is that Catholics believe intercourse is one of the deepest expressions of human love and creativity in marriage. In 1985, the Irish bishops issued a pastoral letter on the issue entitled "Love Is for Life." The letter affirms the role of sex as an important part of marital love:

> Sexual union is only one part of the total language of sexuality.... a special moment in a whole conversation of love between husband and wife. This conversation is carried on by words, by letters, by signs and by silences...acts of thoughtfulness, attentiveness, remembrance and concern. Above all, it includes real commitment to sharing life together "for better, for worse, for richer, for poorer, in sickness and in health...." Sexual union without this context is flawed by doubt and uncertainty. It carries a lie at its heart.

Not only is sex a physically and emotionally unifying act in the context of marriage, but it also holds the opportunity for sharing in God's creativity by procreation. This language of love that brings the couple pleasure and joy and provides them with creative potential combine the two "fruits" or purposes of marriage.

Prayer for My Spouse
Lord Jesus, grant that my spouse and I may have a true and understanding love for each other. Grant that we may both be filled with faith and trust. Give us the grace to live with each other in peace and harmony. May we always bear with one another's weaknesses and grow from each other's strengths. Help us to forgive one another's failings and grant us patience, kindness, cheerfulness and the spirit of placing the well-

being of one another ahead of self. May the love that brought us together grow and mature with each passing year. Bring us both ever closer to you through our love for each other. Let our love grow to perfection. Amen.

Prayer for Marriages

Christ, who blessed the wedding at Cana with an abundance of new wine, bless our marriages. We pray for the marriages of our parents that brought us into the world, for the marriages of our friends and family members, and for our own future marriages. May these marriages be joyful and lifegiving. May they be animated with a love that reflects your love for us: a never-ending love, an unconditional love, a self-sacrificing love, an exclusive love. May the Holy Spirit, give all married couples the grace to grow in love, to raise their children to be good citizens of heaven and earth, to weather all trials and conflicts, and finally to celebrate love with you forever in the great wedding feast of heaven.

9. Holy Things and Places

ost of us, as human beings, are blessed with five senses; concrete things and actions speak to us. Catholics use objects to touch our hearts and minds so that our faith increases and our relationship with God deepens. Sacramentals are ordinary physical items with symbolic purpose or meaning that have been blessed by a priest. Backed by the prayers of the Church, they become channels of grace for us. There are many different sacramentals that help us connect our physical existence with an invisible God:

Blessed ashes	Holy oil	Religious statues
Blessed candles	Holy water	Rosaries
Blessed palm	Incense	Scapulars
Crucifixes	Prayer books	Stations of the Cross
Holy cards	Relics of saints*	Votive lights
Holy medals	Religious pictures	

Blessings, a Sacramental

Did you know that "good-bye" is a short form of a blessing? It means "God be with you." Blessings are prayers over someone or something to seek God's favor, small wishes of abundance and peace in our lives. There are blessings for almost anything. Although rosaries, medals, and prayer books are often taken to a priest to be blessed, anyone can give a blessing. Some parents have the beautiful custom of blessing their children before they go to bed—and asking them for a blessing in return.

There are three kinds of relics: pieces of a saint's body (first class); objects sanctified by close contact with a saint in life (second class); and items that have been touched to a first-class relic (third class).

Expecting a blessed medal to ward off danger is superstitious. The medal is a sign of our faith, not a magic object. The prayers and good living which the medal inspires us to are the real sources of its power.

Recipe for a Blessing

Begin your blessing with the Sign of the Cross over a person or item being blessed; you might use holy water or holy oil to do so. Consider the intention of the blessing, and say a prayer incorporating that theme or purpose. You might extend your hand or hands toward the person, place your hand or hands on the person's head, or hug the person as you're praying for them. Another option is sprinkling the person or item with holy water. When someone prays over you or offers a blessing, respond by making the Sign of the Cross and concluding with "Amen."

Extraordinary Blessings

❖ On February 2 the Church celebrates the feast of the Presentation when Simeon acknowledged Jesus as the light of the Gentiles. On this day, candles that will be used by the Church during the year are blessed.

❖ On February 3 we celebrate the feast of St. Blase, a bishop who saved a boy from choking on a fishbone. We come to church to have our throats blessed. Two candles are tied with ribbons to form a cross. They are held to each person's neck as a prayer for protection against all throat ailments is prayed.

❖ October 4 is the feast of St. Francis, known for his rapport with animals. In his honor, some parishes invite people to bring their pets to church for a blessing.

A Blessing from the Bible (Numbers 6:24-26)

May the Lord bless and keep you;
the Lord make his face to shine upon you
*   and be gracious unto you;*
The Lord lift up his countenance upon you
*   and give you peace.*

Icons, an Eastern Sacramental

An icon is a highly stylized and ornate painting of Christ, Mary, or a saint. This style of religious art—one rich in symbolism—began in the Byzantine churches. The process of painting an icon is itself a very spiritual exercise, involving prayer and fasting. To the Eastern churches an icon is like a sacrament: God is present in the painting itself.

Holy Places

A *church* is the house of God where God's family assembles to pray and to offer the sacrifice of the Mass. Center stage in the church is the *altar* where Jesus is offered to the Father. Near it is the *ambo*, or lectern, from which the Word of God is proclaimed. The altar, lectern, and crucifix are in the space called the sanctuary. The *tabernacle*, where the Blessed Sacrament is housed, is located either there or in a special room of adoration. A *sanctuary light* burns constantly to signal God's presence in the tabernacle. The *baptismal font,* where new members are initiated, is located near the doors in the back to symbolize entrance into the Church, or near the altar to show Baptism's relationship with the Eucharist. Somewhere in the church is a *Reconciliation room* or confessional where God forgives repentant sinners. Stained-glass windows, pictures, and statues in the church remind us of our faith and inspire us to pray.

In addition to a parish church, there are other houses of worship that have distinct features and so are called by different names. The usually large and majestic main church of a diocese where the bishop presides is called a *cathedral*. Also, another huge place of worship is a *basilica*, a church that has special historical or religious meaning. A *chapel* is a small church, usually within a larger institution,

trivial tidbit...

Saying "God bless you" when someone sneezes is a blessing that originated in 600 A.D. At that time, an epidemic was plaguing Italy. The main symptom was severe sneezing. Pope Gregory the Great issued a decree making "God bless you" the response to a sneeze.

An indulgence is the remission of the temporal (as opposed to eternal) punishment our sins deserve after they've been forgiven. Indulgences are either plenary (remitting all punishment) or partial. Certain prayers and actions gain indulgences as prescribed by the Church, using the merits of Jesus and the saints. Indulgences can be applied to oneself or to the souls in purgatory. You may see indulgences expressed as a number of days, meaning they are equivalent to that many days of penance. The prayers, devotions, and religious acts to which indulgences are attached can be found in a book called the Raccolta. In the sixteenth century, some Church members sold indulgences, a scandal that helped lead to the Reformation.

such as a hospital, school, or even an airport. A *shrine* is a church or sacred place where people come on pilgrimage and may obtain indulgences.

The Land Holy to Christians, Jews and Muslims

Most of salvation history was set in the country Israel, the land to which God led Abraham and Sarah and the Promised Land to which Moses led Egypt's Hebrew slaves. This is also the native land of Jesus where he lived and died, going from town to town teaching the Good News.

Israel lies on the east shore of the Mediterranean Sea. (It is roughly the size of Vermont.) Palestine, the eastern section of Israel, has three parts: Galilee in the north, Samaria in the middle, and Judea in the south. Jesus was born in Bethlehem and died in Jerusalem, both in Judea. He lived in Nazareth and later Capernaum, both of which are in Galilee. Samaria was home to the Samaritans, Jews who had been left behind during the Babylonian captivity and had intermarried with non-Jews.

The Sea of Galilee in the north has been called the most beautiful sea in the world. It played a large role in the life of Jesus. He sailed over it, taught from it, calmed its waves, drew fish from it, and walked on its waters. The Dead Sea in the south is the lowest point on the Earth and is filled with salt. These two seas are connected by the 125-mile-long Jordan River in which Jesus was baptized, accepting his mission.

Highlights of a Holy Land Tour

❖ **Bethany**: The tomb of Lazarus is right on a street in the town. It is reached by going down stone steps and crawling through a small, short tunnel. Nearby is the Church of Lazarus that has

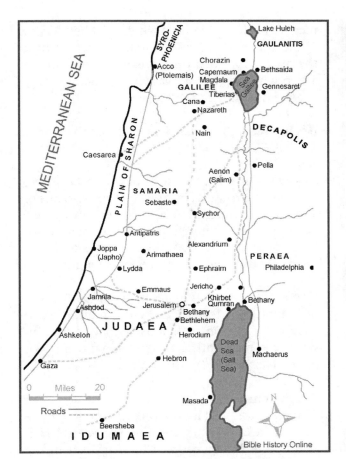

Bible History Online

for your
spiritual
health...

Consider making a pilgrimage to the Holy Land at least once in your life. You'll never hear the Bible stories in the same way after you've walked the land where Jesus and his people lived. If a trip is not possible, settle for a video, slides, or a picture book of Israel.

"I am the resurrection and the life" above the altar and mosaics of scenes of Jesus with Lazarus, Mary and Martha.

❖ **Bethlehem**: The City of David is five miles southwest of Jerusalem in the hill country of Judea. The Basilica of the Nativity, located on Manger Square, dates back to 530 A.D. and is built on the site of the first church constructed in the first half of the fourth century. Appropriately, you must stoop to enter its low doorway. In a cave in the lower level of the church, a silver star marks the place of Jesus' birth. East of Bethlehem is the Shepherd's Field Church, marking where the angels appeared on Christmas night. Inside are bright frescos of Nativity scenes. Nearby shepherds still tend their sheep.

❖ **Bethsaida**: Jesus healed a blind man here. (See Mark 8:22-26.)

❖ **Capernaum**: The house thought to be where Peter lived is found here as well as the remains of a Byzantine church. They are covered by a large, circular, modern church built by the Franciscans. Ruins of a synagogue nearby possibly stand over the original synagogue where Jesus taught.

❖ **Cana**: Three large churches commemorate Jesus' first miracle performed at Mary's request. Each church is a different religious denomination. Inside the Roman Catholic church is a mosaic floor dating back to the fourth century.

❖ **Ein Karim**: In this town stands the beautiful Church of the Visitation. Walking into it you see a lovely fresco of Mary meeting her relative Elizabeth. The Church of John the Baptist is in the center of town. In the grotto of the church under an altar is a star that marks where John the Baptist was born.

❖ **Gallicantu**: The Church of St. Peter is on the supposed site of the house of Caiaphas the High Priest, traditionally where Peter denied his Master. Steps in its courtyard date back to the time of Jesus. When he was here, astronaut Neil Armstrong—the first man to walk on the moon—commented, "This is where the real giant leap for mankind took place."

A Parable of Two Seas

Two seas lie in Palestine. In the north is the Sea of Galilee. Its fresh, blue waters teem with fish; trees spread their branches over it and stretch out roots to sip its waters; along its shores children play. Jesus could look across its silver surface as he taught. People build their homes near it, and birds their nests; and every kind of life is happier because it is there. The Jordan River makes this sea with sparkling water from the hills. The Jordan River flows on south into another sea. Here there is no splash of fish, no fluttering leaf, no song of birds, no children's laughter. Travelers choose another route. Dead trees coated with salt jut out of it. The air hangs heavy above it, and no creature drinks its brackish waters filled with mineral deposits. What makes the difference in the seas? The Sea of Galilee receives but does not keep the Jordan. For every drop that flows into it another drop flows out. The other sea gives nothing. It is named the Dead Sea.

—Bruce Barton (adapted)

fyi...

From what we know of first-century Palestine, we deduce that Jesus spoke Aramaic, and knew some Hebrew for prayer. He also may have known some Greek. His name, Jesus, was a Greek translation of the Hebrew name Joshua, probably *Jeshua*.

❖ **Gerasa**: This town is in Jordan. Here Jesus cast out demons from swine, and the Gerasenes, frightened at his power, asked him to leave (See Mark 5:1-20).

❖ **Jericho**: Perhaps the oldest city in the world, Jericho was taken by the Israelites—led by Joshua—as they entered the Promised Land. In the parable of the Good Samaritan, the traveler was on the way to Jericho from Jerusalem. Just west of Jericho is the Mount of Temptation, which has a chapel marking where Satan tempted Jesus. On the side of the mountain is a Greek Orthodox monastery.

❖ **Jerusalem**: A two-and-a-half-mile wall with eight sets of gates surrounds this small city. The Golden Gate, or Beautiful Gate on the eastern wall is traditionally where Jesus passed through on Palm Sunday; Jewish tradition states that Messiah will pass through that gate. It has been walled up since the ninth century. The Citadel, King Herod's fortress, adjoins the Jaffe Gate.

The center of attraction in Jerusalem is the Dome of the Rock, a mosque built on the site of the Jewish temple. Inside and on the top of Mount Moriah is a rock sacred to three great religions: Jews and Christians revere it as the place where Abraham was ready to sacrifice Isaac and where the Ark of the Covenant stood in the Temple; for Muslims it is the rock from which Mohammed ascended to heaven. The mosque is richly decorated in red and gold with brilliant mosaics. Not far from this mosque for individual prayer is the Mosque of El-Aksa, where Muslims hold group worship.

In Jerusalem you can also visit the Upper Room where it is thought that Jesus ate the Last Supper and the Holy Spirit came upon the apostles on Pentecost Sunday.

The western (or wailing) wall in Jerusalem is all that remains of the Jewish temple. Jewish people as well as pilgrims slip papers with prayer intentions between its massive stones. Hulda Steps excavated in the southern wall lead into the courtyard and date back to the time of Jesus. In Jerusalem, too, is the Church of the Dormition where, according to tradition, Mary fell into eternal sleep. A wooden and ivory effigy depicts her on her deathbed.

❖ **Via Dolorosa:** Stations of the Cross recall Jesus' passion. Nine of them are on the street amidst the hubbub of the market place, and five are within the Church of the Holy Sepulcher. The Church of the Holy Sepulcher is built over Calvary or Golgotha, where Jesus died. There, you can visit the Stone of Anointing where Jesus presumably was prepared for burial. This same church also houses the tomb of the resurrection. (Outside the walls of Jerusalem is the Garden Tomb that many Protestants identify as Christ's.) In addition, the nearby Chapel of the Lithostrotos (paved square) is within the Antonia Fortress where Pontius Pilate judged Jesus; in the courtyard, markings are still visible where the Roman soldiers played games like the Game of Kings.

❖ **Magdala**: Mary Magdalene, a disciple of Jesus and witness of the crucifixion, was from this town. Later the risen Lord appeared to her and sent her to tell the apostles the Good News of his resurrection.

❖ **Mount of Olives**: The Garden of Gethsemane, where Jesus prayed the night before he died, overlooks Jerusalem. Some of the olive trees have been there for centuries. In the garden, the Church of All Nations (Basilica of the Agony) is built over a large rock said to be the one Jesus prayed on in the garden. An iron crown of thorns circles the rock as a memorial to Christ's sacrifice. Also on the Mount of Olives and facing Jerusalem is the Church of Dominus Flevit (the Lord Cries), marking where Jesus wept over the city of Jerusalem. On top of the Mount of Olives is the octagonal Chapel of the Ascension that houses a rock on the spot where Jesus ascended to the Father.

During a draught in 1985, a sunken boat was discovered in the Sea of Galilee that is thought to be a fisherman's boat dating back to the time of Jesus—1 B.C. to 70 A.D.

❖ **Mount Tabor**: The Basilica of the Transfiguration stands on top of this high mountain. Above its altar is a glorious, gold mosaic showing Christ with Moses and Elijah, Peter, James and John.

❖ **Nain**: Jesus met a funeral procession in this city and brought the widow's son back to life.

❖ **Nazareth**: In this, the Holy Family's hometown, pilgrims can draw water from the only spring in town at the Church of St. Gabriel, just as Mary must have done two-thousand years ago. An old synagogue stands where Jesus may have read Scripture. At the Church of St. Joseph is the grotto of the Holy Family, which may have been Joseph's workshop. Also in Nazareth is the enormous Basilica of the Annunciation that contains artwork of Mary from different countries. Inside is an altar that claims, "Here the Word was made flesh."

❖ **Qumran**: In 1947 a shepherd boy discovered manuscripts more than two-thousand years old in a cave in Qumran. A religious community, the Essenes, apparently stored them in a cave when they fled from the Romans. Called the Dead Sea Scrolls, the manuscripts are housed in the Shrine of the Book at the Israel Museum in Jerusalem.

❖ **Sea of Galilee**: "Jesus boats" take tourists across this harp-shaped sea, where they may experience the strong winds described in the Gospels. Overlooking the Sea of Galilee and atop the Mount of Beatitudes is the Church of the Beatitudes, an octagonal structure marking the spot where Jesus gave us the eight beatitudes.

❖ **Tabgha**: The Church of the Multiplication of the Loaves and the Fishes, built in the fourth century, commemorates Jesus' feeding the multitude. On its floor in front is a mosaic of the loaves and the fishes. Not far from the church is the Church of the Primacy of St. Peter. It is built on a large rock on the shore of the Sea of Galilee. The rock called *Mensa Christi,* meaning "Table of Christ," is within the church. Outside stands a statue of Jesus saying to Peter, "Feed my sheep." Beside the church ancient steps lead to the water.

a cool website...

For a tour of St. Peter's Basilica go to www.ewtn.com/gallery/sp/sp1.htm.

The Holy City: Rome

Rome, called the eternal city, is considered the heart of the Roman Catholic Church; holy popes have lived there, and martyrs have died there.

❖ **The Basilica of St. Peter** in the Vatican City is the largest church in the world, and the site of the major ceremonies of the Catholic Church. Enormous statues of Christ, John the Baptist, and the apostles line its roof. Inside, under its mosaic-covered dome and beneath Bernini's famous canopy of twisted columns, is the papal altar. Directly below the altar is St. Peter's tomb along with the tombs of other popes, and below that is an ancient cemetery. The basilica houses Michelangelo's Pietà (Mary holding the lifeless body of Jesus) and a huge bronze statue of St. Peter, whose foot has been worn away by pilgrims' touches. Visitors who have the stamina can climb the steps to the dome and look out over Rome.

❖ **St. Peter's Square,** the courtyard outside the Basilica of St. Peter, has a grand double colonnade of 284 columns and statues of 140 saints. The colonnade's two arms seem to embrace the

At first Greek was spoken in the Church. Then Latin became the official, universal language of the Catholic Church and used in the liturgies around the world. Since the Second Vatican Council, Mass has been prayed primarily in the language of the people.

pilgrims who gather there for religious functions such as the papal blessing. In the center of the square stands a pink Egyptian obelisk.

❖ **The Vatican Museums and Art Gallery** contain what is considered the greatest collection of ancient archeological exhibits and works of art in the world.

❖ **The Vatican Library** houses one of the largest collections of rare books. Its walls are decorated with precious masterpieces by famous artists.

❖ **The Sistine Chapel** is the site where cardinals meet to elect a new pope. In silence, visitors gaze at its ceilings covered with Michelangelo's dazzling frescos of Bible scenes and the wall behind the altar that bears his awesome scene of the Last Judgment.

❖ **The Basilica of St. John Lateran,** the cathedral of the Diocese of Rome, was the residence for the pope until 1305. Inside the basilica, colossal statues of all the apostles stand in niches along the central part of the church. The **Holy Stairs** across the street are believed to be those Jesus climbed on the way to his trial. Pilgrims make a painful climb on their knees.

❖ **St. Callistus catacombs** and **St. Sebastian catacombs** are the underground cemeteries for many early Christians. Tombs are carved into their high walls.

❖ **The Colisseum** once seated fifty-five thousand spectators and had seventy-six entrances. Today a plain stark cross stands as a reminder of the many Christians martyred there.

134

- ❖ **The Pantheon,** a pagan temple, was consecrated as a Catholic church in 609. It has an amazing dome and contains the tomb of the artist Raphael.

- ❖ **Circus Maximus** used to be an enormous stadium where the Romans held races and killed Christians for sport.

- ❖ **The Basilica of St. Mary** houses the tombs of St. Catherine of Siena and Fra Angelico, a fifteenth century Dominican painter.

- ❖ **St. Peter in Chains Church** contains the chains that supposedly bound Peter in prison and it is the site of Michelangelo's *Moses* statue.

- ❖ **The Basilica of St. Mary Major** was built in the fourth century after a miracle of summer snow in 352 A.D. and a vision of Mary. Inside are spectacular mosaics. The basilica's bell tower is one of the tallest in Rome.

- ❖ **The Basilica of St. Paul Outside the Walls** was originally built by Constantine, about a mile from where Paul was martyred. Today on its walls are mosaic portraits of every pope.

- ❖ **Tre Fontane Abbey,** home of the Trappist monks, is near the site where Paul was beheaded.

- ❖ **The Domino Quo Vadis Church** on the Appian Way (a famous road on which St. Paul was led a prisoner to Rome) is named for the question Jesus asked Peter when he was fleeing Rome: "Where are you going?"

- ❖ **The Basilica of Santa Maria** in Trastevere may be the oldest Christian building in Rome.

The church Santa Maria della Concezione has a crypt below where the skeletons of 4,000 Capuchin monks decorate the ceilings and walls of chambers. Skulls and other bones are piled to form walls and arches, and some have been fashioned into patterns such as hearts and crowns of thorns. At the exit is posted, "What you are, we used to be, what we are, you will be." The site is a macabre but creative reminder of the afterlife.

❖ **Castel Sant' Angelo** built in 136 A.D., a mausoleum for emperors, at different times became a fortress, a prison, and a residence for popes. It was named for St. Michael the Archangel whom St. Gregory the Great saw in a vision as he led a procession over the San Angelo Bridge to end the plague. The San Angelo Bridge over the Tiber River leads to Vatican City. It is lined with angels holding the instruments of Our Lord's passion.

❖ **The Basilica of St. Clement** is built over a fourth century church, which is built on the site of ancient Roman buildings.

❖ **The Arch of Constantine** was erected in 315 A.D. in honor of the emperor Constantine, who guaranteed religious freedom with the Edict of Milan.

10. What's God Calling You To?

Each of us has a mission to complete while we are on Earth. God calls everyone to be holy—that is, to love as he loves. This is our primary call. God not only calls us to holiness, but God calls us each to travel a certain lane. On the road to holiness these are the options: married life, single life, ordained life, or religious life. We call these states of life *vocations*, from the Latin word for "call." All four vocations are important and complement the others. Which one is right for you?

Your challenge is to identify the path that is most life-giving for you, the one that matches the gifts and talents you've been given—the one God has in mind for you. You owe it to God, to the Church, and to yourself to explore *all* the options and then carefully make the best decision you can.

To help determine your vocation, consider using the discernment process described on page 144 ff. and pray the vocation prayers in this chapter. Also, pray that others may have the courage to answer God's call—especially the call to be a priest, brother and sister religious. (The dwindling number of these religious vocations weakens the life of the Church.) Abundant living for us as individuals and for the Church as a whole depends on how open we are to God's call and how faithfully we follow it.

Prayer of Affirmation

I am loved by God; I am made by God;
I am forgiven by God; I am accepted by God unconditionally;
I am a child of God; I am sustained by God;
I am important to God; I am used by God.
I am enabled by God; I am destined for God.

Read these stories
about some famous
"calls" in salvation
history.

Abraham and Sarah—
Genesis 12:1-6; chap-
ters 15, 17, 18

Moses—Exodus 2-4

Samuel—1 Samuel
3:1-10

David—1 Samuel 16:
1-12

Isaiah—Isaiah 6

Mary—Luke 1:26-56

Disciples—Mark 1:
16-20

Paul—Acts 9:1-25

Prayer of Service

(John Henry Cardinal Newman)
*God has created me
to do him some definite service.
He has committed some work to me
which he has not committed to another.
I have my mission—
I may never know it in this life;
but I should be told it in the next.
I am a link in a chain,
a bond of connection between persons.
He has not created me for naught.
I shall do good.
I shall do his work.
I shall be an angel of peace,
a preacher of truth in my own place
    while not intending it—
if I do but keep his commandments.
Whatever, wherever I am, I can never be thrown away.
If I am in sickness, my sickness may serve him.
He does nothing in vain.
He knows what he is about.
    He may take away my friends;
    he may throw me among strangers;
    he may make me feel desolate,
    make my spirits sink,
    hide my future from me—
still he knows what he is about.
Therefore, I will trust him.*

Vocation Prayer

(Thomas Merton)
*My Lord God, I have no idea where I am going.
I do not see the road ahead of me.
I cannot know for certain where it will end.
Nor do I really know myself,
and the fact that I think that I am following your will
does not mean that I am actually doing so.*

138

But I believe that the desire to please you does in fact
please you.
And I hope I have that desire in all that I am doing.
I hope that I will never do anything apart from
that desire.

And I know that if I do this,
you will lead me by the right road though I may know
nothing about it.

Therefore will I trust you always
though I may seem to be lost and in the shadow
of death.
I will not fear, for you are ever with me,
and you will never leave me to face my perils alone.

St. Francis of Assisi's Vocation Prayer:
Most High, Glorious God, enlighten the darkness of our
minds. Give us a right faith, a firm hope and a perfect
charity, so that we may always and in all things act
according to your Holy Will. Amen.

WORDS TO LIVE BY
❖ "If you deliberately plan to be less than you are
capable of being, then, I warn you that you'll be
unhappy for the rest of your life. You'll be evad-
ing your own possibilities."**—Abraham
Maslow**

❖ "Let no one mislead you or prevent you from
seeing what really matters. Turn to Jesus, listen to
him, and discover the true meaning and direction of your lives."**—Pope John Paul II**

❖ "God has not called me to be successful; he has
called me to be faithful."**—Blessed Teresa of
Calcutta**

You dare your yes and
experience meaning.
You repeat your yes
and all things acquire
a meaning.
When everything has a
meaning, how can you
live anything but a
yes?
  —Dag Hammarskjöld

139

❖ "Work as though everything depends on you; pray as though everything depends on God." —attributed to **St. Ignatius of Loyola**

❖ "When we have accepted the worst, we have nothing more to lose. And that automatically means—we have everything to gain."—**Dale Carnegie**

❖ "Whatever you do, do it well, and you have praised God."—**St. Augustine**

❖ "Do all the good works you can while you still have the time."—**St. John of God**

❖ "If a man does not keep pace with his companions, perhaps it is because he hears a different drummer. Let him step to the music which he hears, however measured or far away."—**Henry David Thoreau**

❖ "Growth begins when we start to accept our own weakness."—**Jean Vanier**

A Guide to Vocations

Every vocation has the same two goals: personal growth in holiness and fruitfulness. Each one, however, has unique characteristics and makes a unique contribution to the life of the Church.

Religious life is a lifestyle that involves total commitment to the Church. (The ordained life of diocesan bishops, priests, and deacons is discussed on page 117 ff.) In religious order vocations, men (priests and brothers) and women (sisters) are consecrated to God. They make vows (usually vows of poverty, chastity, and obedience), live in community, and follow a Rule or way of life originally outlined by a founder. Each congregation has a *charism*, a special gift for the Church that characterizes them as a whole and as individuals and permeates its mission. For example, St. Dominic's community promotes the intellectual life of the Church through preaching and teaching. There are two types of religious. *Active* or *apostolic religious* serve God's people, especially the poor, as Jesus did. Among other things, they are teachers, missionaries, parish staff members, and social service providers. *Contemplative religious* serve by praying and doing penance for the Church while staying enclosed in their convents or monasteries. As they grow in love for God and others, religious bear fruit through their ministries and their prayer.

In **married life,** a man and a woman become holy through their commitment to each other and to the children with whom they may be entrusted through procreation or adoption. In their wedding vows, a couple promises among other things to love and care for each other "in sickness and in health" until they are separated by death. They are unified in their mission as Catholics, acting as "one body." Their vocation means more than having sexual relations only with one's spouse—the definition of chastity in marriage. It involves being fully present in the marriage, being vulnerable and merciful in relationship to another flawed person. Personal growth occurs when married persons strive for virtue as the partner of another person and the leader of a family. Fruitfulness in marriage is the children the couple has the potential to produce, although not all are given this mission. Married persons also bear fruit as they work in businesses, the home, or the Church, and as they encourage the other family members to grow in faith.

Some men and woman are called to be **single and chaste** and to serve the world through a ca-

"The harvest is abundant but the laborers are few; so ask the master of the harvest to send out laborers."
—Luke 10:2

141

cool
websites...

Most religious communities have their own websites. You can find the website for the Sisters of Notre Dame at www.sndchardon.org. You can find information about many other religious communities at www.visionguide. org.

reer, caring for family members, and being in relationship with other people. This is how they are best able to achieve personal growth: by using their gifts and loving friends and neighbors. The fruit of the single life is the varied work single people do as well as the lives they touch along the way.

Seeking Fidelity

Attaining the goals of personal growth and fruitfulness in any of these vocations takes fidelity. Priests and religious men and women need to be faithful to their commitment to God, the Church, and their vows. Married people need to be faithful to each other by keeping their marriage vows. Single people are called to be faithful to their lifestyle of loving and serving the community at large. Success in life is proportional not to how much money we make or how important our work is, but to how faithful we are to living our lifestyle.

Associates

A growing phenomenon in religious communities is an *associate* program. Associates are lay persons—male or female, married or not—who are attracted to a community's spirit and ministry and wish to be part of it. They do not take vows but go through a formation program and share in the prayers and works of the community. Associates are sometimes called *affiliates* or *third order members.*

Secular Institutes

A comparatively new Church opportunity is the *secular institute*. This is an organization where the members take private vows and live and work on their own rather than in community. Their mission is to infuse the workplace with the gospel of Christ. Periodically, members of a secular institute gather for meetings and retreats.

Missionaries

Men and women who take the Word of God and the love of Jesus to other countries or to underserved areas of the country are called missionaries. You might consider spending a year or two—or the rest of your life—being a missionary. Visit www.maryknoll.org to learn about one Catholic missionary organization, or contact your diocese for information about others.

Remember that whether or not you become a profesional missionary, we are all sent by Christ to evangelize, spreading the Good News of our faith.

Church Ministries

Did you ever think about a career serving the Church? The pay may not be terrific, but the retirement plan is out of this world—eternal life!

You might become a:

❖ missionary in a foreign country
❖ missionary in your country (home missionary)
❖ youth minister or campus minister at a high school or college
❖ pastoral minister at a parish
❖ teacher in a Catholic school
❖ director of religious education at a parish
❖ employee at a parish or a diocesan office
❖ employee of a Catholic organization
❖ writer/editor/publisher of Catholic literature

quick quote...

Love cannot remain by itself—it has no meaning. Love has to be put into action and that action is service.
    —Blessed Mother
    Teresa of Calcutta

Think about some of the gifts and interests you have. How could you use those gifts to serve God and the Church?_____

_____

_____

_____

143

Catholic Organizations

Join one of the many Catholic organizations for the laity. There are many regional, diocese-based, national and international organizations. Here are some of the better known national and international lay Catholic organizations. Does your parish or diocese have a chapter?

❖ Knights of Columbus—A fraternal benefit society of Catholic men that has more than a million and a half member who do apostolic works (www.kofc.org)
❖ St. Vincent de Paul Society—An organization whose main goal is to carry out the works of mercy (www.svdpusa.org)
❖ Daughters of Isabella—A fraternal order for women (www.daughtersofisabella.org)
❖ Holy Name Society—A group that promotes reverence for the Holy Name of Jesus (www.holynamesociety.info)
❖ National Center for the Laity—A group that promotes the vocation of the laity in and to the world (www.catholiclabor.org/NCL.htm)
❖ The Christ Child Society—A group dedicated to serving at-risk children regardless of race or creed (www.nationalchristchildsoc.org)
❖ Serra International—An organization that fosters vocations to the priesthood and religious life (www.serrainternational.org)

How to Choose a Vocation

As you go through life, you make countless choices: what to wear, what cereal to eat for breakfast, what movie to see on Friday night. Some decisions are weightier than others, those that strongly impact your life and the lives of others: where to go to college, what career to pursue, what state of life to follow, or whom to marry. Because God has a plan for you and he is your all-wise maker, you will want to listen for God's guidance as you decide what to do. This Christian process of decision-making is called *discernment*. Discernment is the art of finding God's will in the situations which confront you. Here are ten key components of the discernment process:

1. **Get to know yourself.** What are your interests? Gifts? Limitations? Deepest desire?
2. **Assess** whether your proposed action is compatible with Scripture, Church tradition, and your values.
3. **Gather information** by reading and using the Internet.
4. **Get advice** from professionals, family members, relatives, and friends.
5. **List the pros and cons** of each vocation, and then evaluate them. Be aware that the shorter list might outweigh the longer one.
6. **Pay attention to your feelings** and intuition. What does your heart tell you to do?
7. **Consider the alternatives.**
8. **Pray** in quiet solitude. Discuss the decision with Jesus. Ask his help. Consider how your decision will affect your relationship with him. Listen. What do you hear God saying?
9. **Trust yourself,** your memories, and your past decisions.
10. **Imagine** how the decision will affect you five years from now, twenty-five years from now.

Ask Yourself ...
❖ What are my motives?
❖ Am I free to accept or reject the options?
❖ How does my choice align with my priorities?
❖ If I were on my deathbed, which choice would I wish I'd have made?
❖ How would I advise a friend in my shoes?

A Test:
Imagine you have made the choice. How does it feel? Are you comfortable with it? Is there peace or restlessness? (Peace of mind indicates that you have chosen wisely.)

11. You've Got Mail: The Bible

The Bible is the Word of God in the words of human beings. It puts us into contact with God. At the beginning of time God's mighty word brought forth all creation out of nothing. Likewise, when Jesus, who is God, spoke, great things happened. His word cured people, forgave sins, calmed storms, and brought the dead to life. Now this same word of God is available to us in the Bible, a book that is the last word on abundant life.

Although they were written for a particular people at a particular time in history, the books of the Bible still are rich in meaning for us. Why? Mainly, because the Spirit of God is alive in it and in us. Moreover, the Bible tells the story of our faith, and its writers are inspired by God. It is the basis of our beliefs as Catholic Christians and our roadmap for our spiritual journey in this life. Scripture provides us with wisdom and advice when we face difficult decisions; encourages us in hard times; and celebrates God's glory, mercy and love with us on page after page.

The Bible wasn't made to sit in a drawer or to collect dust on a bookshelf; rather, the divine revelation its pages hold is intended to be part of our daily lives as we "walk by faith." God speaks personally to each of us through Scripture today just as strongly as he did thousands of years ago. Our job is to stop (open our Bible) and listen.

THE BIBLE: A LIBRARY

The Church, guided by the Holy Spirit, determined the list (canon) of the seventy-three books in the Bible at the Council of Trent in 1546. Catholics follow the Greek translation, the Septuagint. This version has more books in the Old Testament than the Hebrew Scriptures that the Protestant and Jewish people accept as divinely inspired. Catholics call these additional "Catholic" books *deuterocanonical* ("second canon") books, while Protestants call them *apocryphal*. There are many literary genres in the Bible. You'll find historical books, prophetic books, stories, poetry, and even a love song!

What Bible to Get?

If you are looking for a Bible, find a Catholic version so that you have all the books included in the Catholic canon. Some popular Catholic translations include the New American Bible (the translation used for Mass), the New Revised Standard Version, the New Jerusalem Bible, and the more traditional Douay-Rheims Bible written in English that is more than four-hundred years old.

Reading the Bible

Reading the Bible is a form of prayer. We connect with the grief, pain, anxiety, hopelessness, trust, and joy in a biblical story or psalm; and we sit in wonder. We read a Gospel story about Jesus and are moved to express thanks, praise and love. The Bible brings God's saving grace into our lives. Throughout the ages, men and women have experienced the perfect Bible quotation coming into their awareness at just the right moment. One man who found the Bible to be his saving grace was Terry Anderson. Held hostage in Lebanon for nearly seven years, he read the Bible cover-to-cover fifty times—a prayer that helped him survive.

BOOKS IN THE BIBLE

Old Testament

Pentateuch
Genesis
Exodus
Leviticus
Numbers
Deuteronomy

Joshua
Judges
Ruth

Historical Books
1 Samuel
2 Samuel
1 Kings
2 Kings
1 Chronicles
2 Chronicles
Ezra
Nehemiah
Tobit
Judith
Esther
1 Maccabees
2 Maccabees

Wisdom Books
Job
Psalms
Proverbs
Ecclesiastes
Song of Songs

Wisdom
Sirach

Prophetic Books
Isaiah
Jeremiah
Lamentations
Baruch
Ezekiel
Daniel
Hosea
Joel
Amos
Obadiah
Jonah
Micah
Nahum
Habakkuk
Zephaniah
Haggai
Zechariah
Malachi

New Testament

Gospels
Matthew
Mark
Luke
John

Acts of the Apostles

Letters
Romans
1 Corinthians
2 Corinthians
Galatians
Ephesians
Philippians
Colossians
1 Thessalonians
2 Thessalonians
1 Timothy
2 Timothy
Titus
Philemon
Hebrews

Catholic Letters
James
1 Peter
2 Peter
1 John
2 John
3 John
Jude

Book of Revelation

cool websites...

You can read the New American Bible version of Scripture at www.vatican.va/archive/ENG0839/_INDEX.HTM. Go to www.biblegateway.com to locate a certain passage or word.

The Wild West gang *J. T. Web and the two McCabes* will help you remember the deuterocanonical books that Catholics consider divinely inspired: Judith, Tobit, Wisdom, Ecclesiastes, Baruch, 1 and 2 Maccabees (along with parts of Esther and Daniel).

The Bible, however, can seem like an overwhelming book at first. The thick spine and tiny print may leave one wondering where to begin. There is no one "right" way to read the Bible. Some choose to read the Bible like a book, while others marinate in single verses. Do you want to try a few strategies for reading Scripture? Find John 11—the death of Lazarus. First, read the story all in "one bite," John 11:1-44. As you read the passage, consider what strikes you about the story. Think about the characters and what is happening in the story. Now, try going back and sitting with verse 35, "Jesus began to weep." Those four little words have an incredibly rich implication. Reflect on that verse and each

JUST FOR FUN
Everything I need to know about life I learned from Noah's Ark.

One: Don't miss the boat.

Two: Remember that we are all in the same boat.

Three: Plan ahead. It wasn't raining when Noah built the Ark.

Four: Stay fit. When you're six-hundred years old, someone may ask you to do something really big.

Five: Don't listen to critics; just get on with the job that needs to be done.

Six: Build your future on high ground.

Seven: For safety sake, travel in pairs.

Eight: Speed isn't always an advantage. The snails were on board with the cheetahs.

Nine: When you're stressed, float a while.

Ten: Remember, the Ark was built by amateurs; the Titanic by professionals.

Eleven: No matter the storm, when you are with God there's always a rainbow waiting.

–Author Unknown

word. Try to envision Jesus weeping. Each of these ways of reading the Bible has its own beauty. The point is not how you are reading the Bible but that you do so. It is also helpful to use a Bible that has commentary included beside the passages or with a study aid that can give the context of and insight into the stories. Here are other some other strategies for reading Scripture:

The Bible was the first book printed on Johannes Gutenberg's printing press in 1457. Since then this bestseller of all time has been translated into more than 2,500 languages.

- ❖ Keep your Bible on your pillow or beside your bed, and read one or two lines every night before you go to sleep. What will happen? After two lines you'll think, "I can read a few more." Before you know it, you'll have read a whole book!
- ❖ Read an entire book, such as the Gospel of Mark, in one sitting—similar to the way you'd read a novel you just couldn't put down.
- ❖ Choose one book in the Bible and read only the section headings in boldface print. Then reflect on the impact of the whole.
- ❖ Read according to a theme: prayer, faith, forgiveness, justice, women, trees. Look up your theme in a *concordance*, a reference book that lists words and where they can be found in the Bible. You can also use your Bible's index or cross-references to locate verses.
- ❖ Follow the church Lectionary by reading the selections that will be used the following Sunday. Consider using a lectionary-based devotional or reflection materials to help you throughout the liturgical year.
- ❖ Write comments or prayers in the margins of your Bible. Underline, highlight, or star verses that speak to you.

A Personal Letter

The Bible is like a love letter from God to you. It is meant to be taken personally. If you read it with

Did you know that there is a version called the *Wicked Bible?* In the story of the woman caught in adultery Jesus tells her, "Go sin no more." The typesetter of the *Wicked Bible* accidentally left out one little word in that phrase: No!

faith, expecting God to speak to you, you will hear God. This is not superstition but an act of faith. Here are ways to use the Bible as instant communication with God and to personalize it:

❖ **The Lucky Dip** (or Bible Roulette!): Open the Bible at random and read the lines your eyes first fall on. St. Francis called this way of seeking God's word as the First Opening. He used this method to find rules for his community, the Franciscans. St. Augustine also experienced the power of random reading. One day he heard a child's voice chanting, "Take and read." When he picked up the Bible, he read the verses that changed his sinful life to a saintly one. (Romans 13:13–14)

❖ **Birthday Gift:** On your birthday go to Mass and listen to the readings for a special gift from God. If you can't wait, look up the readings for the day in a Lectionary.

❖ **Adapting the Text:** Read the verses aloud and insert your name into them or substitute your name for pronouns in a passage.

❖ **Paraphrasing**: Rewrite a psalm or other biblical prayer in your own words. The Magnificat and Psalm 23 lend themselves to this activity.

❖ **Updating**: Read a Gospel story, then rewrite it as though you were there; arrange the plot in the end so that you are alone with Jesus. Then write a conversation you have with him about what just happened.

Love Notes

St. Gregory the Great says: "Scripture enables us to know the heart of God through the word of God." The Bible reveals that God's heart is full of love for us. Prayerfully consider each of these verses that God says to you in Scripture:

❖ "Can a mother forget her infant, be without tenderness for the child of her womb? Even should she forget, I will never forget you" (Isaiah 49:15).

❖ "I have grasped you by the hand" (Isaiah 42:6).

❖ "I will espouse you to me forever... and you shall know the Lord" (Hosea 2:21).

❖ "I have called you by name; you are mine" (Isaiah 43:1).

a cool website...

Find the Sunday readings and short reflections at *Word of Life* online at www.catholicnews.com/word2lif.htm

BIBLE QUESTIONS FOR YOU TO ANSWER

Read questions in the Bible as though God were asking them of you. Answer God!

What are you looking for? (John 1:38)
Do you want to be made well? (John 5:6)
Why are you afraid, you of little faith? (Matthew 8:26)
Who do you say that I am? (Matthew 16:15)
Do you also wish to go away? (John 6:67)
What do you want me to do for you? (Luke 18:41)
Those who believe in me, even though they die, will live. Do you believe this? (John 11:25-26)
Will you lay down your life for me? (John 13:38)
Do you now believe? (John 16:31)
Why are you weeping? (John 20:15)
Do you love me? (John 21:16)

❖ "You are precious in my eyes and glorious, and I love you" (Isaiah 43:4).

❖ "I have carved you on the palms of my hands" (Isaiah 49:16).

❖ "Though the mountains leave their place and

153

Join a Bible study group or start one. This is a very popular way of learning, reading and reflecting on Scripture with friends or other Christians. Bible study resource books, available at your local Catholic bookstore, can guide you through a particular book or themed study. Also, many parishes have regular Bible studies. Check your parish bulletin!

the hills be shaken, my love shall never leave you" (Isaiah 54:10).

❖ "With age-old love I have loved you" (Jeremiah 31:3).

❖ "Anyone who loves me will keep my word, and my Father will love him and we shall come to him and make a home in him" (John 14:23).

❖ "Remember, I am with you always" (Matthew 28:20).

Praying the Psalms
In the center of the Bible lies the prayer book of the Old Testament: the Book of Psalms. These 150 psalms originally were sung by the Jewish people—including Jesus, Mary, and Joseph. Another name for the book of Psalms is the Psalter, a word from the Greek word for "lyre" or "harp." The Jewish people call this book Praises because most psalms are prayers of praise. Psalms are also the basis for many of our modern hymns. You might write your own psalm or piece together favorite lines from existing ones to create a new psalm.

A Psalm to the Wind of Heaven
(Edward Hays)
Wind of Inspiration, Creative Spirit of God,
teach me not to forget
that you come always as gift.
Remind me always to be ready
to receive and romance and dance with joy
wherever and whenever you visit,
or risk that you may move on without me.
May I ever be sensitive to your gentle breezes
and willing to soar with your wild winds.

WORDS ON THE WORD

"You can only understand the Bible on your knees."
                                        —Maurice Zundel

"The Bible is alive, it speaks to me; it has feet, it runs after me; it has hands, it lays hold on me."
                                        — Martin Luther

"In the sacred books the Father who is in heaven comes lovingly to meet his children and talks with them."
                                        —Constitution on Divine Revelation, 21

"Most people are bothered by those passages in Scripture which they cannot understand; but as for me, I always notice that the passages in Scripture which trouble me most are those which I do understand."
                                        —Mark Twain

PSALM VERSES FOR ALL OCCASIONS

- ❖ **In trouble:** "Save me, O God, for the waters have come up to my neck. I sink in deep mire, where there is no foothold" (Psalm 69:1-2).
- ❖ **On happy days:** "Awake, my soul! Awake, O harp and lyre! I will awake the dawn. I will give thanks to you, O Lord, among the peoples" (Psalm 57:8–9).
- ❖ **In the face of death:** "You show me the path of life. In your presence there is fullness of joy; in your right hand are pleasures forevermore" (Psalm 16:11).
- ❖ **When undertaking a new project:** "Let the favor of the Lord our God be upon us, and prosper for us the work of our hands—O prosper the work of our hands!" (Psalm 90:17).
- ❖ **After God answers a prayer:** "Blessed be God, because he has not rejected my prayer or re-

155

Lord, when I found
your words, I devoured
them. They became
my joy and the happi-
ness of my heart.

—Jeremiah 15:16

moved his steadfast love from me" (Psalm 66:20).

❖ **When being persecuted:** "Let those be turned back and brought dishonor who desire my hurt" (Psalm 40:15).

❖ **On getting old:** "Do not cast me aside in my old age; as my strength fails, do not forsake me" (Psalm 71:9).

❖ **In need:** "Restore us, O God of hosts; let your face shine, that we may be saved" (Psalm 80:7).

❖ **For protection:** "When they call to me, I will answer them; I will be with them in trouble, I will rescue them and honor them" (Psalm 91:15).

❖ **In awe at God:** "Make a joyful noise to the Lord, all the earth; break forth into joyous song and sing praises" (Psalm 98:4).

Lectio Divina

One prayerful way to read Scripture is *lectio divina,* which means "sacred reading." It originated in a time when literacy was not prevalent in monasteries. The monks would gather, and someone would read Scripture. Whenever a monk heard a phrase that appealed to him, he would leave the group to ponder and pray over it. There are four steps to *lectio divina,* paralleled to Jacob's ladder reaching heaven (Genesis 28:10–19).

1. *Lectio* (reading). Slowly read the passage, pausing when a word or a phrase stands out. Repeat the word(s) and let it sink into you. Savor it. In this step you put the reading into your mouth just as a grape is placed in the winepress. Soon you will wonder why this verse has grabbed your attention and what it might mean for you. This moves you into the next step.

2. *Meditatio* (meditating). Wrestle with the word, seeking its meaning for your life. Let the word penetrate you. You don't have to keep repeating it, just concentrate on its meaning. This step is like pressing the grape, drawing the juice that will ferment into wine. Remember that vintage wine takes time. At some point you will realize what the word means for you. This is the "Aha!" moment when you are deeply moved and become ready to respond.

3. *Oratio* (praying). Let your prayer move from mind to heart. Talk to God about that word. What response does the word call forth from you—Praise? Thanksgiving? Sorrow? Peace? Commitment? Enthusiasm? Conviction? Stay with those feelings in loving silence, letting yourself desire God and letting God desire you. Put yourself at the disposal of God's Spirit, preparing for God's action. Focus on God. If you feel it is time to return to the reading, do so.

4. *Contemplatio* (contemplating). Contemplation is described as a simple loving gaze, the highest form of prayer. Be alone with God in the great silence that is too deep for words, and let God take over your faculties. You have a direct experience of God. Listen to what God says to you about the word, and enjoy the experience.

The goal of *lectio divina* is this last step: union with God. It may seem as if nothing is happening; this is deceptive. A morsel of Zen wisdom sheds light on this step: "Sitting still/ doing nothing, Spring comes/ and the grass grows by itself."

Notice that the first three steps involve *doing*, but the last step entails simply *being*. The first three steps in *lectio divina* move from words to the fourth step, which is wordless. These four steps can occur in any order and last any length of time. You may repeat steps several times or just do one. You may

Ignorance of Scripture is ignorance of Christ.
—St. Jerome

go back to the passage and read it until another word strikes you. Over time, *lectio divina* forms a listening heart in us so that we become more reflective and more attuned to God in everyday events.

Prayers Lifted from Scripture

The Bible contains some ready-made prayers. Here is a sampling:

One-Liners

❖ "I believe. Help my unbelief" (Mark 9:24).
❖ "If you choose, you can make me clean" (Mark 1:40).
❖ "Lord, save me!" (Matthew 14:30).
❖ "The Lord gave, and the Lord has taken away; blessed be the name of the Lord" (Job 1:21).
❖ "Increase our faith" (Luke 17:5).
❖ "Speak, Lord, for your servant is listening" (1 Samuel 3:10).
❖ "Jesus, Master, have mercy on us!" (Luke 17:13).
❖ "Lord, to whom can we go? You have the words of eternal life" (John 6:68).
❖ "My teacher, let me see again" (Mark 10:51).
❖ "My Lord and my God!" (John 20:28).

Canticle of Zechariah

Blessed be the Lord, the God of Israel;
he has come to his people and set them free.
He has raised up for us a mighty savior,
born of the house of his servant David.
Through his holy prophets he promised of old
that he would save us from our enemies,
from the hands of all who hate us.
He promised to show mercy to our fathers
and to remember his holy covenant.
This was the oath he swore to our father Abraham:
to set us free from the hands of our enemies,
free to worship him without fear,

holy and righteous in his sight all the days of our life.
You, my child, shall be called the prophet
    of the Most High,
for you will go before the Lord to prepare his way,
to give his people knowledge of salvation by the
    forgiveness of their sins.
In the tender compassion of our Lord
the dawn from on high will break upon us,
to shine on those who dwell in darkness and the
    shadow of death,
and to guide our feet into the way of peace.

Psalm 23

The Lord is my shepherd;
I shall not want.
He makes me lie down in green pastures;
He leads me beside still waters;
He restores my soul;
He leads me in right paths for his name's sake.
Even though I walk through the darkest valley,
I fear no evil;
For you are with me;
Your rod and your staff—
They comfort me.

You prepare a table before me
In the presence of my enemies;
You anoint my head with oil;
My cup overflows.
Surely goodness and mercy shall follow
All the days of my life,
And I shall dwell in the house of the Lord
My whole life long.

A Prayer of Trust (Habakkuk 3:17–19)

For though the fig tree blossom not
    nor fruit be on the vines,
Though the yield of the olive fail

Psalm 8 has the distinction of being the first psalm on the moon. When U.S. astronauts landed there in 1969, they left a silicon disk with messages from 71 nations including Pope Paul VI reading of Psalm 8.

159

An educated person is expected to be knowledgeable about the Bible, which has influenced our music, art, literature, and even our language. Which of the expressions below do you think originated in the Bible?

- The handwriting on the wall
- The patience of Job
- Can a leopard change its spots?
- A scapegoat
- As old as Methuselah
- Sour grapes
- The blind leading the blind
- A good Samaritan
- Salt of the earth
- Nothing new under the sun

(Answer: All of them!)

and the terraces produce no nourishment,
Though the flocks disappear from the fold
and there be no herd in the stalls,
Yet will I rejoice in the Lord
and exult in my saving God.
God, my Lord, is my strength;
he makes my feet swift as those of hinds
and enables me to go upon the heights.

De Profundis: Out of the Depths (Psalm 130)

Out of the depths I cry to you, Lord;
Lord, hear my cry!
May your ears be attentive
to my cry for mercy.
If you, Lord, mark our sins,
Lord, who can stand?
But with you is forgiveness,
and so you are revered.

I wait with longing for the Lord,
my soul waits for his word.
My soul looks for the Lord
more than sentinels for daybreak,
let Israel look for the Lord,
for with the Lord is kindness
with him is full redemption,
And God will redeem Israel
from all their sins.

12. A Potpourri of Prayer Practices

An old sea captain was caught in a terrible storm. He did everything he could to save the ship. Finally, as a last resort, he fell on his knees and prayed, "O God, I haven't bothered you for twenty years. Save me, and I won't bother you for another twenty!" Clearly this man did not understand prayer! The traditional definition of prayer is *lifting the mind and heart to God*. St. Paul exhorts us, "Pray without ceasing" (1 Thessalonians 5:17). It sounds as if we are to think of God, talk to God, and be aware of God's presence all day long! (Realistically, you'll probably want to aim to pray somewhere in between the sea captain's idea and Paul's.)

WHAT'S PRAYER?

It is almost impossible to paint a picture of what prayer looks like. Every person prays differently. There are many styles, types, intentions and purposes of prayer. Ultimately, however, prayer mirrors our relationship with God. Prayer has been described as resting our head on the heart of God, enjoying the company of a friend, and wasting time gracefully. Here is how a few holy people answered the simple question, "What is prayer?"

❖ "Prayer is a conversation with one whom you know loves you." **—St. Teresa of Avila**

❖ "Prayer is not playing with a pussycat, but going into the cave of a tiger."**—Archbishop Anthony Bloom**

161

Jesus was a man of prayer. He prayed alone and with others, by night and by day. He prayed before crucial events and spontaneously in the course of everyday affairs. He prayed the psalms at home and in the synagogue. Jesus taught his followers to pray with confidence and with persistence. Read Jesus' advice for praying in Matthew 6:5–13, Matthew 7:7–11, Luke 11:5–8, Luke 17:11–19, Luke 18:2–8, John 16:23.

❖ "Prayer is our humble answer to the inconceivable surprise of living."—**Abraham Heschel**

❖ "Prayer is simply being with God and knowing it."—**Bishop Kenneth Untener**

❖ "Certain thoughts are prayers. There are moments when, whatever be the attitude of the body, the soul is on its knees."—**Victor Hugo**

❖ "Prayer requires more of the heart than of the tongue."—**Adam Clarke**

❖ "God speaks in the silence of the heart. Listening is the beginning of prayer."—**Blessed Teresa of Calcutta**

Letter to Jesus
Writing a letter to Jesus is a form of prayer that helps minimize distractions. Begin "Dear Jesus" and then let your thoughts flow, saying whatever is on your mind. Then sign the letter "Love" and your name. Begin a second letter with "Dear" and your name. Write this letter as though Jesus were writing to you. Do not force the thoughts; they will come. Just let your pen go by itself. Later, read your letters. What do they tell about you and your relationship with Jesus?

Meditation, Ignatian-Style
Choose a Gospel story. Ask for a particular grace and pray that you will make a good meditation; then read the story. Pretend you are a movie director and recreate the story in your mind, filling in details that appeal to the senses. What do you see at the scene? hear? taste? feel? smell? What are the people saying? What do they look like? Then analyze the story by asking questions: Who? What?

When? Why? Next, ask how the story applies to your life. At some point during the meditation, have a colloquy—a heart-to-heart talk—with Jesus. Make a resolution for action, pray for the grace to keep it, and thank God for the grace of the meditation. You might take away a thought from the experience and "nibble" on it for the rest of the day.

a cool website...

The Irish Jesuits have a popular website named Sacred Space that guides people through prayer every day. For a spiritual treat, go to www.sacredspace.ie.

A few good stories to reflect on with this kind of prayer:

Calling the first disciples	Luke 5:1–11
Raising the daughter of Jairus	Mark 5:21–43
Healing of a leper	Luke 5:1–11
Healing of a paralyzed man	Luke 5:17–26
The sinful woman	Luke 7:36–50
Calming the storm	Luke 8:22–25
Blessing the children	Luke 19:15-17
Miracle of the loaves	John 6:1–13
Walking on the water	John 6:16–21
Zacchaeus	Luke 19:1–10
The rich young man	Matt. 19:16–22
Blind Bartimaeus	Mark 10:46-52
The Last Supper	Luke 22:14–23
The agony in the garden	Luke 22:39–46
The crucifixion	Luke 23:33–49
Journey to Emmaus	Luke 24:13–35

Centering Prayer

Centering prayer is a simple way of praying that is founded on the belief that God dwells within us. John of the Cross said, "O soul, most beautiful of creature who longs to know where the beloved is, you yourself are the very tabernacle where he dwells." The easiest way to get in touch with God is to go into our heart of hearts. This is what we do in centering prayer. We block out everything else and focus on God living in us, using a short prayer word to keep us centered on God. The following are the steps for centering prayer:

1. **Quiet yourself and relax.** Sit upright so your head is supported by your spine. Gently close your eyes, breathe slowly—exhale, take in fresh air, hold it, and exhale again. Focus on your breathing for a while to help calm your mind.
2. **Move toward God.** Center your consciousness on God dwelling deep within you. Ponder God's love for you, and let God's overwhelming love and goodness draw you. Be present to God, simply resting in God's presence.
3. **Respond with a word or phrase** such as *I love you,* or *My Lord and my God*—or simply the name of *Jesus.* Repeat this prayer word slowly in your mind.
4. **Enjoy God's presence.** Focus on giving God your loving attention. If you find your mind drifting to other things use your prayer word as a hook to bring you back. Don't stop to think about how you're doing!
5. **Pray a prayer.** At the end pray an *Our Father* or other prayer to make the transition out of centering prayer.

Mantras: Prayer of the Heart

Are there days when you feel too tired or worried to pray? A *mantra* might be just the prayer you need—a short prayer that is repeated over and over. The repetition of the word can be as calming as ocean waves or the movement of a rocking chair. Your mantra might come from a favorite prayer, from Scripture (such as the Psalms), or from the Mass prayers. You can also come up with your own mantra. Perhaps if you are feeling overwhelmed your mantra could be a simple "Help." The Lord doesn't need eloquent prose in order to know your heart; find a way to express your sentiments. You might pray the mantra silently or aloud—or even sing it. You can also synchronize the words with your breathing. As you say the word, listen with love and desire.

a cool website...

You can listen to Christian radio online at www.klove.com. K-Love radio not only has stations in cities across the country, but also streams their broadcasts so listeners can enjoy great Christian music around the globe. They also have information on the top Christian songs, concerts and artists.

Some suggested mantras

- ❖ Jesus.
- ❖ I give you thanks, O Lord, with my whole heart.
- ❖ My God, I love you.
- ❖ Blessed are you, Lord.
- ❖ You have the words of eternal life.
- ❖ My Lord and my God!
- ❖ Most Sacred Heart of Jesus, I place my trust in you.
- ❖ You alone are the holy One.
- ❖ My God, how good you are.
- ❖ Lord, I adore you.
- ❖ Abba.
- ❖ You are my all.
- ❖ My Jesus, mercy.
- ❖ Speak, Lord, for your servant is listening.
- ❖ Lord, you are my strength and my might.
- ❖ I believe, my Lord; help my unbelief.
- ❖ You, Lord, are my light and my salvation.

You can also pray a *reverse mantra,* words that Jesus/God says to us in Scripture:

- ❖ "Be still and know that I am God" (Psalm 46:10).
- ❖ "Do not fear, for I am with you" (Isaiah 41:10).
- ❖ "I am the good shepherd" (John 10:11).
- ❖ "With everlasting love I will have compassion on you" (Isaiah 54:8).
- ❖ "I am the resurrection and the life" (John 11:25).
- ❖ "I will strengthen you, I will help you" (Isaiah 41:10).
- ❖ "I am with you always" (Matthew 28:20).

fyi...

Gregorian chant, or plainsong sung during worship particularly in monasteries, is the oldest chant still in use. Chants dating from the sixth century are believed to be the work of Pope Gregory I from whom the name comes. Recently, Gregorian chant has had a resurgence of popularity among the laity as well, spawning the release of several chant CDs.

quick quote...

Pray as you can and do not try to pray as you can't. Take yourself as you find yourself; start from that.
—Dom Chapman

Music to Pray By

Some religious songs by contemporary musicians are so lively they'll have you snapping your fingers and tapping your feet to the beat. Some are so catchy you'll be humming them all day. Others are so beautiful they'll move you to tears. You can listen to religious music on a Christian radio station or on your own CD player, singing along with the songs and making them your prayers. This style of worship may inspire your own prayers—you may even compose a song yourself.

Are you unsure about which contemporary Christian music artist to listen to? Your best bet is to head to your local Christian bookstore. What are some of your favorite styles of music? Chances are there is an array of Christian artists who play that particular style of music. A good start is a compilation of worship songs by different artists to give you a taste of what's out there. You can also sing religious hymns of the past, as they are part of our Catholic heritage.

Also, check to see if any parishes or monasteries near you have nights of Taizé prayer—a popular form of chant written by the monks of Taizé in France. Short mantras and prayers are sung over and over as a kind of musical meditation.

Prayer Springing from Anything

Creation is God's handiwork. You've probably had the experience of witnessing an awesome sunset or standing on a shore where waves were crashing or flying in a plane and looking down on the world. When we behold wonders like these, our heart naturally soars up to God. Actually, anything can lead us to think of God and respond with praise, thanks, petition, contrition, or love. One way to inspire prayer is to use an object as a springboard: a pencil, a penny, a seashell, a rock. Look at it and reflect on

166

its characteristics, its use, its history. What does it say to you about God, your relationship with him, or your life? Talk to God about it, even if just for a moment.

United We Stand: Group Prayer

Praying with someone else or with a group has a particular dynamic about it. Jesus explained, "Where two or three are gathered in my name, I am there among them" (Matthew 18:20). Our spiritual selves are bolstered by joining with other believers to address God. Communal prayer reminds us that we are part of the Body of Christ, the communion of saints. Shared prayer can happen in groups of millions, such as World Youth Day; in smaller groups like the many prayer groups that meet in parishes and communities; and with a single person, such as a friend or loved one.

Shared prayer is a rich and spiritually abundant experience. It reminds us that faith is not something we "hide under a bushel basket" but instead share because it is catholic or "universal." Shared prayer also deepens our understanding of God. None of us can ever fully comprehend God; however, we experience hints of God every day in our world, in our faith, and in our relationships. Prayer reveals how individuals relate to God. Some see God as a loving father; others as a king.

What are some words you would use to explain your concept of God? _____

_____

_____

_____

Shared prayer diversifies the language of our prayer by exposing us to the way other people approach God in their personal faith relationship.

In one of Juliana of Norwich's visions, Jesus said to her, "Pray inwardly, even if you do not enjoy it. It does you good, though you feel nothing, see nothing, yes even though you think you are dry, empty, sick or weak. At such a time your prayer is most pleasing to me."

167

Some use elaborately worded prayers, while others use a more childlike vernacular. Praying with others is a simple yet profound way to grow in faith and to widen our spiritual lens.

Shared prayer can seem a little intimidating. Opening your heart to God in the presence of another person makes you vulnerable. Remember, however, that your words are aimed at God, not the person you're praying with. One way to test the waters of shared prayer is joining a prayer group. Your agenda can be as simple as praying the rosary together. If you can't find a prayer group, consider starting one yourself. Also, consider praying with a close friend or loved one on a regular basis. Another possibility is getting a small group together for "conversational prayer"—a style in which people take turns praising God, thanking God, interceding for others, and petitioning God for themselves.

A Labyrinth Meditation

During the Middle Ages Christians often made a pilgrimage to Jerusalem. Those who couldn't make that holy journey walked a labyrinth at one of seven European cathedrals. A labyrinth is not a maze, which has many paths and is meant to confuse. Rather, the labyrinth, usually circular, has an intended path that leads from the outside, through winding turns, to the center (the new Jerusalem), and back again. The one path of the labyrinth is like the journey of life. Today, some Catholics use this meditation as a way of walking with God.

To walk the labyrinth, bring all that you are to the center, to God. Focus yourself at the entrance. Then walk slowly, maybe taking one step with each breath. (Or you might dance, skip, or stop as the Spirit moves you.) Sometimes the path goes away from the center, just as our journey toward God sometimes seems. As you walk, quiet yourself and

cool
websites...

A finger labyrinth can be found at www. lessons4living.com/ finger_labyrinth.htm. For a unique labyrinth experience, go to www.yfc.co.uk/ labyrinth/online.html or www.labyrinthsoci- ety.org/flash/labyrinth. htm.

let go of busyness and control. On the labyrinth you might meet others; make room for them. At the center rest and wait, listening to God within. Then, journey with God back out to share God's love with others.

If there is not a labyrinth near you, copy and en- large the labyrinth design here and "walk" it on paper with your finger. Or on a website that has a labyrinth, use your mouse to walk.

Ideas for walking the labyrinth

* Walk with a Scripture verse, a feeling, a question, a mantra, a need, or simply walk, noticing your thoughts and feelings.
* Walk with adoration, lovingly aware of God.
* Play music or sing.

Journaling—a Journey Within

Our thoughts and emotions hold pieces of us and our faith. Many people have found writing in a journal to be an effective way to get in touch with their deeper selves and with God. A journal is not a diary—a factual record of the year; it is much more. It's a place to go when things go wrong, a means to work through a confusing situation or bewildering feelings—a place where you can be yourself. Journaling can be a source of freedom, relaxation and fun—as well as a gateway to spiritual growth. It can help you own your past and present more fully and face life realistically.

Writing, like prayer, takes discipline. Often the hardest part is showing up. The first step in journaling is doing just this: setting aside time for writing. Get a special book—either a journal you pick up at a bookstore or one you make yourself. Keep it where you will be most likely to make time to journal. To begin journaling, try writing about the day's experiences and your reactions. Let the words flow out of your mind and through your pen. Don't stop to edit or reread; just let the words "happen." Keeping your journal private will help you to be honest. Write anything you wish. You can write poems or simply a few words if you have only a minute or two. Allow God to creep into your deepest anxieties. Occasionally, go back and re-read what you've written and see how much you've grown or changed—or perhaps you might even recognize areas in which you've lost your way.

If you need help getting started, choose a sentence or quotation to reflect upon or pick one of these sentences to lead into your writing meditation:

❖ I feel like a success when …
❖ I am happy when …

170

❖ It makes me angry when …
❖ I wish …
❖ Nothing is as important to me as …

If you aren't sure what to write about, these questions will jumpstart your journaling. Pick one each day, or answer the same questions daily and build on your response.

❖ What do you usually daydream about?
❖ Think of a person in your past. What did he or she mean to you?
❖ Who are your heroes?
❖ What role does religion play in your life?
❖ What is your happiest memory? Your saddest?
❖ What is your chief fault?
❖ What do you get excited about?
❖ What is your most attractive feature? Your least?
❖ What is your favorite image of God?
❖ What is your biggest challenge right now?
❖ What do you think God is saying to you today?

These questions may not seem "spiritual" to you, but in coming to understand yourself more deeply, you ultimately come to know God more intimately. Also, invite Jesus into your reflection, praying that he might help you to see you as he does—lovingly and mercifully.

FIVE PRAYER FACTS

1. A life hemmed in by prayer is less likely to unravel.
2. If you are too busy to pray, you are too busy!
3. Seven days without prayer makes one weak.
4. Prayer changes people, and people change the times.
5. One thing we can pray for is the gift of prayer.

Life is fragile. Handle with prayer.
—Author Unknown

The best test for prayer is not how many good thoughts we get or how holy we feel, but whether it makes us better Christians. Make prayer a habit. Do it at a certain time until you can't resist doing it and you miss it when you don't do it. Try praying while walking, working, shopping, or cooking! Persevere, but don't be disappointed if God doesn't answer your prayer right away. He might have a better idea! (This is what the boy found who used to pray for the gift his uncle had: the ability to take his teeth out every night and put them in a glass of water!)

The Tandem—A Meditation

At first I saw God as my observer, my judge, keeping track of the things I did wrong, so as to know whether I merited heaven or hell when I die. He was out there, sort of like a president. I recognized his picture when I saw it, but I didn't really know him.

But later on when I met Christ, it seemed as though life were rather like a bike—a tandem bike, and I noticed that Christ was in the back helping me pedal. I don't know just when it was he suggested we change places, but life has not been the same since I took the back seat to Jesus, my Lord. Christ makes life exciting. When I had control, I knew the way. It was rather boring and predictable. It was the shortest distance between two points.

But when he took the lead, he knew delightful long cuts, up mountains, and through rocky places and at breakneck speeds; it was all I could do to hang on! Even though it looked like madness, he said, "Pedal!" I was worried and anxious and asked, "Where are you taking me?" He laughed and didn't answer, and I started to learn to trust. I forgot my boring life and entered into adventure. And when I'd say, "I'm scared," he'd lean back and touch my hand.

He took me to people with gifts that I needed, gifts

172

of healing, acceptance, and joy. They gave me their gifts to take on my journey, our journey, my Lord's and mine. And we were off again. He said, "Give the gifts away; they're extra baggage, too much weight." So I did—to the people we met—and found that in giving I received, and still our burden was light.

At first, I did not trust him in control of my life. I thought he'd wreck it, but he knows bike secrets, knows how to make it bend to take sharp corners, jump to clear high rocks, fly to shorten scary passages. And I'm learning to be still and pedal in the strangest places, and I'm beginning to enjoy the view and the cool breeze on my face with my delightful constant companion, Jesus.

And when I'm sure I just can't do any more, he just smiles and says, "Pedal."

—Author Unknown

quick quote...

We go to prayer not because we love prayer but because we love God.
—Herbert van Zeller

13. Devotions
(from the Grassroots)

When we think of devotion, we think of being committed to something we love. We promise love and devotion in wedding ceremonies. Ultimately as Catholics our highest devotion is to the Trinity. The practice of that loving commitment has many popular forms that have evolved through the centuries and are known as *devotions*. The Eucharist is our number one prayer to which nothing can compare. However, there are other devotions that nourish our faith.

The Rosary

Praying the rosary is a sign of love for the Blessed Virgin Mary. The *Hail Mary* is prayed on most of its beads. In apparitions, Mary told us to pray the rosary especially for peace. Beads are used to tally prayers in most of the world religions. Catholics have several kinds of prayer beads called chaplets—the most widely-used one being the rosary. Catholics give rosaries as gifts, hang them their cars, and are buried with them in their hands.

Despite the legend that Mary gave the rosary to St. Dominic, we know that this devotion developed gradually. Outside of the Eucharist, the 150 psalms of the Old Testament were the chief prayer of the early Church, inherited from our Jewish ancestors in the faith. Long ago, however, many people were illiterate. They began to pray the central prayers: the Our Father, the Hail Mary, and the Glory Be in place of the psalms. These prayers became separated into three groups or chaplets, each containing five sets of decades (ten beads). It was a simple way for common Catholics to pray who could not read books.

175

quick quote...

The rosary is my favorite prayer. A marvelous prayer! Marvelous in its simplicity and its depth.
—Pope John Paul II

trivial tidbit...

In the United States, Father Patrick Peyton promoted praying the family rosary and coined the motto "The family that prays together stays together."

While people prayed the prayers, they pondered the mysteries in the life of Christ: joyful, sorrowful, and glorious events. In 2002, Pope John Paul II introduced a fourth set of mysteries, the luminous mysteries or mysteries of light. These mysteries are events from the public life of Jesus, filling in the large gap between the joyful mysteries and the sorrowful ones. You might even compose your own mysteries: the miracle mysteries, the parable mysteries, and so forth.

How to Pray the Rosary

❖ Make the Sign of the Cross using the crucifix.
❖ Pray the Apostles' Creed on the crucifix.
❖ On the introductory beads pray an Our Father, three Hail Mary prayers and a Glory Be.
❖ Then for each decade that follows ...
  • Recall the mystery for the decade.
  • Pray an Our Father on the single bead.
  • Pray Hail Mary prayers on the ten beads.
  • At the end pray the Glory Be.
❖ Optional: After each Glory Be, some people pray the Fatima Prayer: "O my Jesus, have mercy on us, forgive us our sins, save us from the fires of hell. Take all souls to heaven, especially those most in need of thy mercy."
❖ Optional closing prayer: Hail, Holy Queen (See page 35 ff.)
❖ End with the Sign of the Cross.

The Joyful Mysteries

1. The Annunciation

The angel Gabriel was sent by God to Mary in Nazareth. He announced that God had chosen her to be the Mother of Jesus the savior, the Mother of God (Luke 1:26–28).

176

2. The Visitation

Mary visited her older relative Elizabeth who was pregnant with John the Baptist. When Elizabeth heard Mary's greeting, she cried out, "Most blessed are you among women, and blessed is the fruit of your womb." Mary responded with the Magnificat prayer (Luke 1:39–45).

3. The Birth of Jesus

Mary gave birth to Jesus, wrapped him in swaddling clothes, and laid him in a manger. Angels appeared to shepherds and sang, "Glory to God in the highest and on earth peace to those on whom his favor rests" (Luke 2:1–20).

4. The Presentation in the Temple

Mary and Joseph took the baby Jesus to the Temple to present him to God. There, Simeon and Anna recognized Jesus as the Savior (Luke 2:22–38).

5. Finding of the Child Jesus in the Temple

After Passover, twelve-year-old Jesus remained in Jerusalem without his parents' knowledge. Three days later they found him in the temple listening to teachers and asking them questions (Luke 2:41–50).

The Luminous Mysteries

1. The Baptism in the Jordan River

Jesus had John the Baptist baptize him. A voice came from the heavens saying, "This is my beloved Son, with whom I am well pleased" (Matthew 3:17).

2. The Wedding at Cana

When wine ran out at a wedding, Mary appealed to Jesus and he worked his first miracle. He turned water into excellent wine (John 2:1–12).

fyi...

A university student once sat on a train next to an old man praying the rosary. "Do you believe in such things?" the student asked the man. "Yes, I do. Don't you?" asked the man. Laughing, the student said, "I don't believe in such silly things. Take my advice. Throw the rosary out of this window and learn what science has to say." "Science? I don't understand," said the man. "Maybe you can explain it to me." The student offered, "Give me your address and I'll send you some literature." After fumbling in his pocket, the old man drew out his business card. The boy looked at the card and burned with shame. It read, "Louis Pasteur, Director of the Institute of Scientific Research, Paris."

3. *The Proclamation of the Kingdom of God*

Jesus proclaimed the good news of God's love and salvation, saying "This is the time of fulfillment. The kingdom of God is at hand. Repent, and believe in the gospel" (Mark 1:15).

4. *The Transfiguration*

Jesus took Peter, James, and John up to Mount Tabor. While he prayed, his face changed and his clothing became dazzling white. He spoke with Moses and Elijah (Luke 9:29).

5. *The Institution of the Eucharist*

On the night before he was crucified, Jesus shared a meal with his disciples and gave us the Eucharist. He offered himself for us under forms of bread and wine. In the Eucharist he is with us in a special way (Mark 14:22–26).

The Sorrowful Mysteries

1. *The Agony in the Garden*

After the Last Supper, Jesus went to a garden and prayed, "My Father, if it is possible, let this cup pass from me; yet, not as I will, but as you will" (Matthew 26:36–46).

2. *The Scourging at the Pillar*

Pontius Pilate, to satisfy the crowd, had Jesus scourged and handed him over to be crucified (Mark 15:1–16).

3. *The Crowning with Thorns*

Soldiers stripped Jesus and threw a scarlet military cloak about him. They wove a crown out of thorns and placed it on his head, and put a reed in his hand. Kneeling before him, they mocked, "Hail, King of the Jews!" (Matthew 27:27–31).

178

4. The Carrying of the Cross

Jesus, weak from being whipped and beaten, was unable to carry his cross to Golgotha alone. Simon, a Cyrenian, was forced to help him (Mark 15:20–22).

5. The Crucifixion

At Golgotha, Jesus was crucified between two criminals yet said, "Father, forgive them, they know not what they do" (Luke 23:33–46).

The Glorious Mysteries

1. The Resurrection

At Jesus' tomb an angel appeared to two women, saying "Do not be afraid! I know that you are seeking Jesus the crucified. He is not here, for he has been raised just as he said." The angel sent the women to tell the disciples (Matthew 28:1–10).

2. The Ascension of Our Lord

Jesus led his disciples to Bethany. He blessed them, then parted from them and was taken up to heaven (Luke 24:44–53).

3. The Descent of the Holy Spirit

The Holy Spirit, promised by Jesus, came to the Church on Pentecost with signs of fire and wind. The apostles fearlessly went out and proclaimed the good news, and people of every language understood them (Acts 2:1–13).

4. The Assumption of Our Lady into Heaven

Mary at the end of her earthly life was taken up body and soul into heavenly glory.

fyi...

In Fatima, Portugal, in 1915 three children—Lucia dos Santos, Francisco and Jacinta Marto—began having visions. The woman who appeared to the children exhorted them to pray the rosary and to promote devotion to the Immaculate Heart of Mary. On her last visit, the lady called herself Our Lady of the Rosary. As a sign of authenticity of the visions, on October 13, 1917, a crowd of fifty-thousand saw the sun rotate and then appear to plunge to Earth. Fatima is now a place of pilgrimage. Pope John Paul II credited Our Lady of Fatima for his surviving the attack on his life in 1981. Lucia became a Carmelite nun and died in 2005.

At first, pilgrims prayed the stations of the cross in the Holy Land and by this gained a plenary indulgence. In time, people were able to receive the same indulgence by making the stations elsewhere. The stations were originally wooden crosses; then pictures were added.

5. The Coronation of the Blessed Virgin Mary

The holy Mother of God, the new Eve and Mother of the Church, reigns in heaven, where she prays for and cares for the members of Christ.

The Stations of the Cross

You may have seen a living stations reenactment of Christ's passion at your parish during Lent. In this devotion, also known as the Way of the Cross, we move from station to station praying about each event from Jesus being condemned to death to his resurrection. As we trace Jesus' steps through pictures along the Way of the Cross, we meditate on the sacrifice he made out of love for us, and this stirs us to love in return and live in gratitude.

The Franciscan Fathers on their missions pray the following prayers at the stations. At each station this prayer is prayed: *"We adore you, O Christ, and we bless you, because by your holy cross, you have redeemed the world."*

First Station – Jesus Condemned to Death
O Jesus, so meek and uncomplaining, teach me resignation in trials.

Second Station – Jesus Carries His Cross
My Jesus, this Cross should be mine, not yours; my sins crucified you.

Third Station – Jesus Falls the First Time
O Jesus! By this first fall, never let me fall into mortal sin.

Fourth Station – Jesus Meets His Mother
O Jesus! May no human tie, however dear, keep me from following the road of the Cross.

Fifth Station – Simon the Cyrenean Helps Jesus Carry His Cross

Simon unwillingly assisted you; may I with patience suffer all for you.

Sixth Station – Veronica Wipes the Face of Jesus

O Jesus! You imprinted your sacred features upon Veronica's veil; stamp them also upon my heart.

Seventh Station – The Second Fall of Jesus

By your second fall, preserve me, dear Lord, from relapse into sin.

Eighth Station – Jesus Consoles the Women of Jerusalem

My greatest consolation would be to hear you say: "Many sins are forgiven you, because you have loved much."

Ninth Station – Third Fall of Jesus

O Jesus! When I'm weary on life's long journey, be my strength and my perseverance.

Tenth Station – Jesus Stripped of His Garments

My soul has been robbed of its robe of innocence; clothe me, dear Jesus, with the garb of penance and contrition.

Eleventh Station – Jesus Nailed to the Cross

You forgive your enemies; my God, teach me to forgive injuries and forget them.

Twelfth Station – Jesus Dies on the Cross

You are dying, my Jesus, but your Sacred Heart still throbs with love for your sinful children.

quick quote...

Let us be generous with our time in going to meet him in adoration and in contemplation that is full of faith and ready to make reparation for the great faults and crimes of the world.
— Pope John Paul II

Thirteenth Station – Jesus Taken Down from the Cross

Receive me into your arms, O Sorrowful Mother; and obtain for me perfect contrition for my sins.

Fourteenth Station – Jesus Laid in the Sepulchre

When I receive you into my heart in Holy Communion, O Jesus, make it a fit abiding place for your adorable Body. Amen.

Some people add another station:

Fifteenth Station – Jesus Rises

Jesus, fill my heart with hope in your promise of eternal life.

Pope John Paul II's Scriptural Stations

1. Jesus prays in the Garden of Olives. (Matthew 25:36-41)
2. Jesus is betrayed by Judas. (Mark 14:43-46)
3. Jesus is condemned to death by the Sanhedrin. (Luke 22:66-71)
4. Jesus is denied by Peter. (Matthew 26:69-75)
5. Jesus is judged by Pilate. (Mark 15:1-5, 15)
6. Jesus is flogged and crowned with thorns. (John 19:1-3)
7. Jesus carries his cross. (John 19:6, 15-17)
8. Jesus is helped by Simon of Cyrene. (Mark 15:21)
9. Jesus encounters the women of Jerusalem. (Luke 23:27-31)
10. Jesus is crucified. (Luke 23:33-34)
11. Jesus promises to share his reign with the good thief. (Luke 23:39-43)

182

12. Jesus is on the cross, with his mother and disciple below. (John 19:25-27)

13. Jesus dies on the cross. (Luke 23:44-46)

14. Jesus is placed in the tomb. (Matthew 27:57-60)

Eucharistic Devotions

As Catholics, we believe in the *Real Presence*: Jesus is physically present in the Eucharist—bread that has become his body though transubstantiation. It is not at all surprising then that many Catholics have a devotion to the Eucharist—Christ in the flesh. Many people—young and old alike—are drawn to adoring Jesus in the Blessed Sacrament. The sacred host is placed in an often elaborately decorated holder called a *monstrance* and set out for adoration—a ritual called *exposition*. Churches are encouraged to have solemn exposition for an extended period once a year, but some parishes have continuous or *perpetual* exposition so that people can adore Jesus in the Blessed Sacrament any time, day or night. They might even have a Eucharistic procession.

Eucharistic adoration concludes with *Benediction*, when the people are blessed with the Sign of the Cross made by the Blessed Sacrament. Reciting the Divine Praises follows, helping make reparation to God for blasphemy and profanity.

The Divine Praises

Blessed be God.
Blessed be his holy name.
Blessed be Jesus Christ, true God and true man.
Blessed be the name of Jesus.
Blessed be his most Sacred Heart.
Blessed be Jesus in the most Holy Sacrament
of the altar.

trivial tidbit...

Forty hours is a devotion in which the Blessed Sacrament is exposed for three days. In the United States this devotion was popularized by St. John Neumann, the bishop of Philadelphia and the first American man to be canonized (1977).

for your spiritual health...

Make a "holy hour" by praying for one hour before the Blessed Sacrament. This practice arose from Jesus' question to the sleeping apostles during his agony in the garden: "Could you not stay awake with me for one hour?" (Matthew 26:40)

fyi...

A *novena* is nine con-
secutive hours or
days of prayer. The
custom is based on
the nine days the
apostles spent pray-
ing in the upper room
while awaiting the
Holy Spirit. An *octave*
is eight days of
prayer.

trivial tidbit...

The practice of re-
ceiving Communion
on the first Friday of
each month honors
the Sacred Heart of
Jesus and gains spe-
cial graces.

Blessed be the Holy Spirit, the Paraclete.
Blessed be the great Mother of God, Mary most holy.
Blessed be her holy and Immaculate Conception.
Blessed be her glorious Assumption.
Blessed be the name of Mary, virgin and mother.
Blessed be St. Joseph, her most chaste spouse.
Blessed be God in his angels and in his saints.

Devotion to the Sacred Heart

The Sacred Heart of Jesus stands for his infinite love
for us. Devotion to the Sacred Heart means a relationship with and a response to Jesus based on understanding him as a person full of love for us—
prompting us to love in return. While devotion to
the Sacred Heart dates back to the medieval mys-
tics, apparitions of Jesus to St. Margaret Mary in the
seventeenth century rejuvenated the devotion.
June is the month of the Sacred Heart.

Novena Prayer to the Sacred Heart of Jesus

O most holy Heart of Jesus, fountain of every blessing,
I adore you, I love you, and with a lively sorrow for my
sins, I offer you this poor heart of mine. Make me
humble, patient, pure and wholly obedient to your will.
Grant, good Jesus, that I may live in you and for you.
Protect me in the midst of danger; comfort me in my
afflictions; give me health of body, assistance in my
temporal needs, your blessing on all that I do, and the
grace of a holy death.

Enthronement of the Sacred Heart

To show that Jesus rules over a family, a picture or
statue of the Sacred Heart can be officially installed
in a place of honor in a home during a ceremony of
prayers and hymns.

Prayer of St. Gertrude

O Sacred Heart of Jesus! Living and life-giving Foun-

184

tain of eternal life, infinite treasure of the Divinity, glowing furnace of Love! You are my refuge and my sanctuary. O my adorable and lovely savior, consume my heart with that burning fire with which yours is inflamed. Pour down on my soul those graces which flow from your love, and let my heart be so united with yours that our wills may be one, and mine in all things conformed to yours. May your will be the rule both of my desire and of all my actions. Amen.

SHORT PRAYERS

- ❖ Jesus, meek and humble of heart, make my heart like yours.
- ❖ Most Sacred Heart of Jesus, I implore that I may ever love you more and more!
- ❖ Heart of Jesus, burning with love of us, inflame our hearts with love of you.
- ❖ May the Heart of Jesus in the most Blessed Sacrament be praised, adored, and loved with grateful affection, at every moment, in all the tabernacles of the world, even to the end of time.

Divine Mercy

A rather new devotion is to Divine Mercy promoted by St. Faustina. On the day of her canonization in the year 2000, the Holy Father declared the Second Sunday of Easter to be the Sunday of Divine Mercy.

Chaplet of Divine Mercy

This prayer uses the rosary in the following manner: Pray the Our Father, the Hail Mary and the Apostles' Creed. Then on the single bead before each decade pray: *Eternal Father, I offer you the body and blood, soul and divinity of your dearly beloved Son, Our Lord Jesus Christ, in atonement for our sins and those of the whole world.*

Our Lord to St. Faustina: *"Encourage souls to say the Chaplet which I have given to you…. Oh, what great graces I will grant to souls who will recite this chaplet. Through the chaplet you will obtain anything, if what you ask for is compatible with my will…. I want the whole world to know my infinite mercy. I want to give unimaginable graces to those who trust in my mercy. By this novena, I will grant every possible grace to souls."*

For many years the Infant of Prague was a popular devotion to Christ's childhood and kingship. This devotion centered on a small statue of the child Jesus crowned and holding a globe surmounted with a cross. His right hand is raised in blessing. The original statue belonged to a community of Discalced Carmelite Fathers in Prague.

On the ten beads of each decade pray: *For the sake of his sorrowful Passion, have mercy on us and on the whole world.*

Conclude by repeating three times: *Holy God, Holy Mighty One, Holy Immortal One, have mercy on us and on the whole world.*

Exaltation of the Holy Cross Novena Prayer

Jesus, who because of your burning love for us willed to be crucified and to shed your most precious blood for the redemption and salvation of our souls, look down upon us and grant the petition we ask for: (mention intention here). *We trust completely in your mercy. Cleanse us from sin by your grace, sanctify our work, give us and all those who are dear to us our daily bread, lighten the burden of our sufferings, bless our families, and grant to the nations, so sorely afflicted, your peace, which is the only true peace, so that by obeying your commandments we may come at last to the glory of heaven.*

14. Soul Food: A Bunch of Great Prayers

Day by Day
(St. Richard of Chichester)
Thank you, Lord Jesus Christ,
For all the benefits and blessings you have given me,
For all the pains and insults you have borne for me.
Merciful Friend, Brother and Redeemer,
May I know you more clearly,
Love you more dearly,
And follow you more nearly,
Day by day.

Prayer for Peace
(St. Francis of Assisi)
Lord, make me an instrument of your peace.
Where there is hatred, let me sow love;
Where there is injury, pardon;
Where there is doubt, faith;
Where there is despair, hope;
Where there is darkness, light;
Where there is sadness, joy.

O, Divine Master, grant that I may not
so much seek to be consoled, as to console;
to be understood, as to understand;

to be loved, as to love;
for it is in giving that we receive,
it is in pardoning that we are pardoned,
it is in dying that we are born to eternal life.

Prayer of St. Augustine
Breathe in me, O Holy Spirit,
that my thoughts may all be holy.
Act in me, O Holy Spirit,
that my work, too, may be holy.
Draw my heart, O Holy Spirit,
that I love but what is holy.
Strengthen me, O Holy Spirit,
to defend all that is holy.
Guard me, then, O Holy Spirit,
that I always may be holy.
Amen.

Prayer Before the Crucifix
Behold, O kind and most sweet Jesus, before your face I
humbly kneel, and with the most fervent desire of my
soul, I pray and beseech you to impress upon my heart
lively sentiments of faith, hope and charity, true contri-
tion for my sins, and a firm purpose of amendment.
With deep affection and grief of soul, I ponder within
myself and mentally contemplate your five holy
wounds, having before my eyes the words which David
the prophet spoke concerning you: "They have pierced
my hands and my feet; I can count all my bones."

Anima Christi
(St. Ignatius of Loyola)
Soul of Christ, make me holy.
Body of Christ, save me.
Blood of Christ, fill me with love.
Water from Christ's side, wash me.
Passion of Christ, strengthen me.
Good Jesus, hear me.

Within your wounds, hide me.
Never let me be parted from you.
From the evil enemy, protect me.
At the hour of my death, call me.
And tell me to come to you
that with your saints I may praise you
through all eternity.
Amen.

For all that has been—
Thanks!
For all that shall be—
Yes!
   —Dag Hammarskjöld

Prayer for Generosity
(St. Ignatius of Loyola)
Lord, teach me to be generous.
Teach me to serve you as you deserve;
to give and not to count the cost;
to fight and not to heed the wounds;
to toil and not to seek for rest;
to labor and not to ask for reward,
except to know that I am doing your will.

Prayer of Abandonment
(Blessed Charles de Foucauld)
My Father, I abandon myself to you.
   Do with me as you will.
Whatever you may do with me, I thank you.
I am prepared for anything, I accept everything.
Provided your will is fulfilled in me and in all creatures
I ask for nothing more, my God.
I place my soul in your hands.
I give it to you, my God,
with all the love of my heart,
because I love you.
and for me it is a necessity of love,
this gift of myself,
this placing of myself in your hands
without reserve
in boundless confidence
because you are my Father.

*Batter my heart, three-
personed God; for you
As yet but knock,
breathe, shine, and
seek to mend;
That I may rise, and
stand, o'erthrow me,
and bend
Your force to break,
blow, burn, and make
me new.*

—John Donne

Radiating Christ

(John Henry Cardinal Newman)

*Dear Jesus, help me to spread your fragrance
    everywhere I go:
flood my soul with your spirit and life;
penetrate and possess my whole being so utterly
that all my life may only be a radiance of yours.
Shine through me and be so in me
that every soul I come in contact with may feel your
    presence in my soul.
Let them look up and see no longer me, but only Jesus!
Stay with me, and then I shall begin to shine
    as you shine;
so to be a light to others.
The light, O Jesus, will be all from you.
None of it will be mine.
It will be you shining on others through me.
Let me thus praise you in the way which you
    love best—
by radiating you to those around me.
Let me preach you without preaching,
not by my words but by my example,
    by the catching force,
the sympathetic influence of what I do,
the evident fullness of the love my heart bears to you.*

Prayer of Cardinal Newman

*May God support us all the day long
till the shadows lengthen
and the evening comes
and the busy world is hushed
and the fever of life is over
and our work is done —
then in mercy —
may God give us a safe lodging
and a holy rest
and peace at the last.*

St. Patrick's Breastplate

*I bind unto myself today the strong name
  of the Trinity,
by invocation of the same, the Three in One,
  and One in Three.*

*I bind this day to me forever by power of faith
  Christ's incarnation;
His baptism in the Jordan River, his death on the cross
  for my salvation;
His bursting from the spiced tomb, his riding up the
  heavenly way,
His coming at the day of doom; I bind unto myself
  today.*

*I bind unto myself today the power of God to hold
  and lead,
His eye to watch, his might to stay, his ear to harken
  to my need;
The wisdom of my God to teach, his hand to guide,
  his shield to ward;
The Word of God to give me speech, his heavenly host
  to be my guard.*

*Christ be with me, Christ within me,
Christ behind me, Christ before me,
Christ beside me, Christ to win me,
Christ to comfort and restore me,
Christ beneath me, Christ above me,
Christ in quiet, Christ in danger,
Christ in hearts of all that love me,
Christ in mouth of friend and stranger.*

*I bind unto myself today, the strong name
  of the Trinity,
By invocation of the same, the Three in One,
  and One in Three,
Of whom all nature hath creation, eternal Father,*

**big book
search...**

A story about the
judge Samuel as a
boy is a lesson on
prayer. Read it in
1 Samuel 3:1–14.
Our attitude to prayer
should be "Speak,
Lord, for your servant
is listening," and not
just "Listen, Lord, for
your servant is
speaking"!

191

Make a practice of
dropping in at a
church or chapel to
visit Jesus in the
Blessed Sacrament.
It's beautiful just to sit
and be with Jesus for
a while—quite literally,
in the flesh. While
you're there you
might light a candle,
read Scripture, or pray
for a special intention.
Spend the time of
your adoration as you
would with a beloved
friend.

Spirit, Word;
Praise to the God of my salvation,
    salvation is of Christ the Lord!

Learning Christ
Teach me, my Lord, to be sweet and gentle
    in all the events of life,
    in disappointments,
    in the thoughtlessness of those I trusted,
    in the unfaithfulness of those on whom I relied.
Let me put myself aside,
    to think of the happiness of others,
    to hide my little pains and heartaches,
    so that I may be the only one to suffer from them.
Teach me to profit by the suffering that comes across
    my path.
    Let me so use it that it may make me patient,
    not irritable.
    That it may make me broad in my forgiveness,
    not narrow, haughty and overbearing.
    May no one be less good for having come
    within my influence.
No one less pure, less true, less kind, less noble for
having been a fellow traveler in our journey toward
Eternal Life.
As I go my rounds from one distraction to another, let
me whisper from time to time, a word of love to thee.
May my life be lived in the supernatural, full of power
for good, and strong in its purpose of sanctity.
Amen.

Serenity Prayer
(attributed to Reinhold Niebuhr)
God, grant me
the serenity to accept the things I cannot change;
courage to change the things I can;
and wisdom to know the difference.
Living one day at a time;

192

Enjoying one moment at a time;
Accepting hardship as
the pathway to peace.

Taking, as he did,
This sinful world
as it is, not as I
would have it.
Trusting that he will
make all things right
if I surrender to his will.
That I may be reasonably happy in this life,
and supremely happy with
him forever in the next.

Prayer of St. Elizabeth of the Trinity

O my God, Blessed Trinity whom I adore, help me to become utterly forgetful of self, that I may bury myself in thee, as changeless and as calm as though my soul were already in eternity. May nothing disturb my peace nor draw me out of thee, O my immutable Lord! but may I penetrate more deeply every moment into the depths of thy Mystery.

Give peace to my soul; make it thy heaven, thy cherished dwelling place, thy home of rest. Let me never leave thee there alone, but keep me there all absorbed in thee, in living faith, adoring thee and wholly yielded up to thy creative action.

O my Christ, whom I love, crucified by love, fain would I be the bride of thy heart; fain would I cover thee with glory and love thee…until I die of very love! Yet I realize my weakness, and beg thee to clothe me with thyself; to identify my soul with the movements of thine own. Immerse me in thyself; possess me wholly; substitute thyself for me that my life may be but a radiance of thine own. Enter my soul as adorer, as restorer, as Savior!

O eternal Word, utterance of my God! I long to pass

my life in listening to thee, to become docile, that I may learn all from thee. Through all darkness, all privations, all helplessness, I crave to keep thee ever with me and to dwell beneath thy lustrous beams. O my beloved star! So hold me that I cannot wander from thy light.

O "Consuming fire," Spirit of Love! descend within me and reproduce in me, as it were, an incarnation of the Word, that I may be to him another humanity wherein he renews his mystery. And thou, O Father, bend towards thy poor little creature and overshadow her, beholding in her none other than thy beloved Son, in whom thou hast set all thy pleasure.

O my Three, my all, my beatitude, infinite solitude, Immensity wherein I lose myself! I yield myself to thee as thy prey. Merge thyself in me, that I may be immersed in thee until I depart to contemplate in thy light the abyss of thy greatness! Amen.

Litany of Humility
(Cardinal Merry del Val recited daily after Mass)
O Jesus! meek and humble of heart, hear me
From the desire of being esteemed,
From the desire of being loved,
From the desire of being extolled,
From the desire of being honored,
From the desire of being praised,
From the desire of being preferred,
From the desire of being consulted,
From the desire of being approved,
Deliver me, Jesus.
From the fear of being humiliated,
From the fear of being despised,
From the fear of suffering rebukes,
From the fear of being calumniated,
From the fear of being forgotten,
From the fear of being ridiculed,
From the fear of being wronged,

194

From the fear of being suspected,
Deliver me, Jesus.
That others may be loved more than I,
That others may be esteemed more than I,
That in the opinion of the world, others may increase,
and I may decrease
That others may be chosen and I set aside,
That others may be praised and I unnoticed,
That others may become holier than I,
    provided that I may become as holy as I should,
Jesus, grant me the grace to desire it.

An Irish Blessing

May the road rise up to meet you,
May the wind be always at your back,
May the sun shine warm upon your face,
And the rains fall soft upon your fields,
And until we meet again,
May God hold you in the palm of his hand.

Sioux Native American Prayer

O Great Spirit
whose voice I hear in the winds,
and whose breath gives life to all the world,
hear me! I am small and weak.
I need your strength and wisdom.

Let me walk in beauty and make my eyes
ever behold the red and purple sunset!
Make my hands respect the things you have made
and my ears sharp to hear your voice.

Make me wise that I may understand the things you
    have taught my people.
Let me learn the lessons you have hidden in every leaf
    and rock.
I seek strength, not to be greater than my brother,
but to fight my greatest enemy—myself.

fyi...

The Catholic Worker Movement, founded in New York City in 1933 by Dorothy Day and Peter Maurin, is grounded in a firm belief in the God-given dignity of every human person. Today more than 185 Catholic Worker communities are committed to nonviolence, voluntary poverty, prayer, and hospitality for the homeless, exiled, hungry, and forsaken and protest injustice, war, racism, and violence. For more information visit www.catholicworker.org.

short prayer...

*From the unreal lead me to the real;
From darkness lead me to light;
From death lead me to deathlessness.*

—Ancient Native American Prayer

*Make me always ready to come to you
with clean hands and straight eyes.
So when my life fades, as the fading sunset,
my spirit may come to you without shame.*

World Peace Prayer

*Lead me from death to life, from falsehood to truth.
Lead me from despair to hope, from fear to trust.
Lead me from hate to love, from war to peace.
Let peace fill our hearts, our world, our universe.*

196

15. SOS: Prayers for Special Needs

I t seems that we are never more open to God than in our times of need—especially those dark times when it seems there is no hope at all. God is all we have to cling to. Jesus meets us in times when our community becomes divided, in times of great sickness or financial hardship, or when life just seems to spin out of control. "Ask and it will be given to you; seek and you will find; knock and the door will be opened to you" (Matthew 7:7). We also turn to God when others are in need, encouraging them with our prayers.

Prayer for Church Unity
(W.E. Orchard)
O God, you are the light of the world, the desire of all nations, and the shepherd of our souls: let your light shine in the darkness, that all the ends of the earth may see the salvation of our God. By the lifting up of your Cross, gather the peoples to your obedience; let your sheep hear your voice, and be brought home to your fold; so that there may be one flock, one shepherd, one holy kingdom of righteousness and peace, one God and Father of all, above all, and in all, and through all.

Prayer for the United States
(attributed to George Washington)
Almighty God, we make our earnest prayer that you will keep the United States in your holy protection; that you will incline the hearts of the citizens to cultivate a spirit of subordination and obedience to government and entertain a brotherly affection and love for one another and for the fellow-citizens of the

United States at large. And, finally, that you will most graciously be pleased to dispose us all to do justice, to love mercy, and to demean ourselves with that charity, humility, and pacific temper of mind which were the characteristics of the Divine Author of our blessed religion and without which we can never be a happy nation. Grant our supplication, we beseech you, through Jesus Christ our Lord. Amen.

Prayer for Protection

Almighty Father, you are lavish in bestowing all your gifts, and we give you thanks for the favors you have given to us. In your goodness you have favored us and kept us safe in the past. We ask that you continue to protect us and to shelter us in the shadow of your wings. We ask this through Christ our Lord. Amen.

Prayer for the Home

Visit, we beseech you, O Lord, this dwelling, and drive far from it all snares of the enemy; let your holy angels dwell herein, to preserve us in peace; and let your blessing be upon us forever. Through Christ our Lord. Amen.

Motorist's Prayer

Grant me, O Lord, a steady hand and watchful eye
That no one shall be hurt as I pass by.

You gave life, I pray no act of mine may take away
or mar that gift of thine.

Shelter those, dear Lord, who bear my company,
from the evils of fire and all calamity.

Teach me, to use my car for others' need;
Nor miss through love of undue speed
The beauty of the world; that thus I may
with joy and courtesy go on my way.

198

*St. Christopher, holy patron of travelers, protect me
and lead me safely to my destiny.
Amen.*

Prayer for Employment

*God, our Father, I turn to you seeking your divine help
and guidance as I look for suitable employment. I need
your wisdom to guide my footsteps along the right path
and to lead me to find the proper things to say and do
in this quest. I wish to use the gifts and talents you
have given me, but I need the opportunity to do so
with gainful employment. Do not abandon me, dear
Father, in this search, but rather grant me this favor I
seek so that I may return to you with praise and
thanksgiving for your gracious assistance. Grant this
through Christ, our Lord. Amen.*

Prayer for Healing

*Lord, you invite all who are burdened to come to you.
Allow your healing hand to heal me. Touch my soul
with your compassion for others. Touch my heart with
your courage and infinite love for all. Touch my mind
with your wisdom, that my mouth may always proclaim your praise. Teach me to reach out to you in my
need, and help me to lead others to you by my example. Most loving Heart of Jesus, bring me health in
body and spirit that I may serve you with all my
strength. Touch gently this life which you have created,
now and forever. Amen.*

Prayer for Life

*O God, our Creator, all life is in your hands from con-
ception until death. Help us to cherish our children and
to reverence the awesome privilege of our share in creation. May all people live and die in dignity and love.
Bless all those who defend the rights of the unborn, the
handicapped and the aged. Enlighten and be merciful
toward those who fail to love, and give them peace. Let*

Fr. Edward Hays rec-
ommends making the
Sign of the Cross as
you strap your seat-
belt over your heart
and praying, "Wrap
me in your love, O
God, and bless my
journey."

My Jesus, mercy!

To clasp the hands in prayer is the beginning of an uprising against the disorder of the world.

—Karl Barth

freedom be tempered by responsibility, integrity and morality.

For People in Trouble
(St. Anselm)

We bring before you, O Lord, the troubles and perils of people and nations, the sighing of prisoners and captives, the sorrows of the bereaved, the necessities of strangers, the helplessness of the weak, the despondency of the weary, the failing powers of the aged. O Lord, draw near to each; for the sake of Jesus Christ our Lord. Amen.

Facing Aging and Death
(Teilhard de Chardin, S.J.)

When the signs of age begin to mark my body (and still more when they touch my mind); when the ill that is to diminish me or carry me off strikes from without or is born within me; when the painful moment comes in which I suddenly awaken to the fact that I am ill or growing old; and above all at that last moment when I feel I am losing hold of myself and am absolutely passive within the hands of the great unknown forces that have formed me; in all those dark moments, O God, grant that I may understand that it is you (provided only my faith is strong enough) who are painfully parting the fibers of my being in order to penetrate to the very marrow of my substance and bear me away within yourself.

Every once in a while you come across an inspirational piece of writing—perhaps even in a forwarded e-mail. Collect these and reread them periodically. Here's a favorite one that continues to encourage Christians around the world:

Footprints

One night a man had a dream. He was walking along the beach with the Lord. Across the sky flashed scenes from his life. In each scene he noticed two sets of footprints in the sand: one belonging to him, and the other to the Lord. When the last scene of his life flashed before him, he looked back at the footprints in the sand. He noticed that many times along the path of his life there was only one set of footprints. He also noticed that it happened at the very lowest and saddest times in his life. This really bothered him, and he questioned the Lord about it. "Lord, you said that once I decided to follow you, you'd walk with me all the way. But I have noticed that during the most troublesome times in my life, there was only one set of footprints. I don't understand why when I need you most, you would leave me." The Lord replied, "My precious, precious child, I love you and I would never leave you. During the times of trial and suffering, when you saw only one set of footprints, it was then that I carried you."

–Anonymous author

16. Walking the Talk

"I am Catholic." That simple declaration changes everything. "Catholic" is not just something to check in a box to identify your "religious affiliation." We have been branded by the Holy Spirit, by the crazy love of God. When we walk out of church, we are still Catholic, still guided by our faith. As Catholics, we are not called to run away from the world, but rather to embrace it and be a light to it. In Matthew 5:14-16, Jesus exclaims to us: "You are the light of the world. A city built on a hill cannot be hid. No one after lighting a lamp hides it under a bushel basket, but puts it on the lampstand and it gives light to all in the house. The same way, let your light shine before others, so they may see your good works and give glory to your Father in heaven." Our faith impels us to spread the light given to us by the Spirit—the light we personally accepted by our Confirmation. We do this not so much by preaching but by actions. The only way to achieve abundant life is by walking the talk.

Prayer to Christ
(Desiderius Erasmus)
O Lord Jesus Christ, you are the Way, the Truth and the Life. We pray you allow us never to stray from you, who are the Way, nor distrust you, who are the Truth, nor to rest in anyone other thing than you, who are the Life. Teach us, by your Holy Spirit, what to believe, what to do, and how to take our rest.

Learning to Walk
When a lawyer asked Jesus for the secret to eternal life (abundant life!), Jesus retorted, "What does the [Jewish] law say?" In reply, the lawyer quoted Deuteronomy 6:5 and Leviticus 19:18: "You shall love the Lord your God with all your heart, and with all your soul, and with all your strength; and

*He has told you, O
mortal, what is good;
And what does the
Lord require of you
But to do justice, and
to love kindness,
And to walk humbly
with your God?*
—Micah 6:8

your neighbor as yourself" (Luke 10:27). Jesus promised, "Do this, and you will live." Later at the Last Supper, Jesus gave us what he called his new commandment: "Love one another as I have loved you" (John 15:12). These commandments are the spiritual hooks on which is hung everything that living our faith entails. What about celebrating the sacraments? That's one way of expressing your love to and for God. It is also a way to show love for yourself! How about caring for the poor? In doing so, you pass on God's love for you to your neighbor. The commandments to love are the simplest measure we have of how we are following the example of Jesus—the one who is love incarnate.

Loving others can sometimes be a difficult task. Some people seem utterly unlovable to us. Some people we are only able to love well by challenging them in ways that are uncomfortable to us. We see Jesus exercising "tough love" as he interacts with the Pharisees. The Pharisees were convinced that their laws and religious observances were "truth." The idea of the Messiah breaking these laws was unfathomable to them; yet Jesus, whom many were calling the Messiah, did so. He constantly healed on the Sabbath (Matthew 12:1), hung out with sinners and thus became "unclean" according to Jewish law (Luke 7:36-50), and even criticized the Pharisees for their self-righteousness (Luke 11). Jesus loved the Pharisees just as he loves all sinners. That's why he opposed them, hoping to open their hearts to God.

Similarly, we may find it necessary to confront a brother or sister in Christ who is missing the point or missing the mark. (We may even need to have a difficult chat with ourselves. Are we like the Pharisees, putting more weight on religious "rightness" than loving our neighbors?) Do we know someone who is hurting himself or herself, or someone who needs "tough love?" Then there are those who don't love us and those who have hurt us. It takes superhuman effort to reach out with love to these people. Factors other than the people themselves make it difficult to love. At times our own concerns, pressures, and crises tend to make us self-centered so that we forget about loving others (including God). Then there are days so jam-packed with things we must do that we don't take time to love. A challenge that we face as Catholics is knowing how to respond to our call to walk the talk. The good news is that we are not expected to have all the answers but simply to turn to God and the Body of Christ for help.

The Golden Rule

A version of the second great commandment is "Do unto others as you would have them do unto you." In 2003, the J. M. Smucker Company—makers of jams and jellies—ranked first in *Fortune Magazine's* list of best employers. The company's president and co-CEO Richard Smucker explained that their success was due to this standard the company practiced: "treating people the way you want to be treated."

The Ten Commandments of God

When the rich young man asked Jesus what to do to gain eternal life, Jesus replied, "If you wish to enter into life, keep the commandments" (Matthew 19:17). Then the man asked, "Which ones?" and Jesus quoted some of what we know today as the Ten Commandments, or Decalogue (meaning "ten words"). These laws, derived from lists in the books of Exodus and Deuteronomy, were gifts God gave his people so that they may reach human fulfillment. Living by them leads to peace and joy. The first three commandments are ways to show love for God, and the rest spell out ways to show love for

Someday, after we have mastered the winds, the waves, the tides, and gravity, we will harness for God the energies of love, and then, for the second time in the history of the world, man will have discovered fire.
—Teilhard de Chardin

205

Read what love
means in 1 Corinthi-
ans 13:4-13. Substi-
tute your name for
the words "love" and
"it" in the first few
sentences. Are the
statements true?

others. In other words, the commandments are elaborations of the two commandments Jesus identified as the greatest.

1. I, the Lord, am your God. You shall not have other gods besides me.

2. You shall not take the name of the Lord, your God, in vain.

3. Remember to keep holy the Lord's Day.

4. Honor your father and your mother.

5. You shall not kill.

6. You shall not commit adultery.

7. You shall not steal.

8. You shall not bear false witness against your neighbor.

9. You shall not covet your neighbor's wife.

10. You shall not covet your neighbor's goods.

The Beatitudes

At times in our lives, we may encounter difficulty, persecution, or other unpleasant experiences because of our faith. We may find ourselves asking "why" and wondering if our less-trodden path is worth the struggle. Jesus encouraged his disciples in his Sermon on the Mount (Matthew 5:1-12). He gave them the blueprint for abundant life here and eternal life hereafter. We call his eight promises the Beatitudes:

❖ Blessed are the poor in spirit, for theirs is the kingdom of heaven.

❖ Blessed are the meek, for they shall possess the earth.

❖ Blessed are they who mourn, for they shall be comforted.

❖ Blessed are they who hunger and thirst for justice, for they shall be satisfied.

❖ Blessed are the merciful, for they shall obtain mercy.

- ❖ Blessed are the clean of heart, for they shall see God.
- ❖ Blessed are the peacemakers, for they shall be called children of God.
- ❖ Blessed are they who suffer persecution for justice' sake, for theirs is the kingdom of heaven.
- ❖ Blessed are you when men reproach you, and persecute you, and speaking falsely, say all manner of evil against you, for my sake. Rejoice and be glad, for your reward in heaven is great.

Wisdom is knowing what to do. Skill is knowing how to do it. Virtue is doing it.
  —Thomas Jefferson

A Love List: Works of Mercy
"Faith apart from works is dead" (James 2:26).

Loving like Jesus means having compassion, expressed through mercy. We extend the mercy to our neighbors that God has given us through Jesus' sacrifice. Works of mercy are our way of "paying it forward" since we could never repay God for all he has done for us. Performing works of mercy results in peace and joy—characteristic of abundant life. An added benefit is that when we practice them, our witness draws others to Jesus.

Corporal Works of Mercy are ways of showing charity by meeting the physical needs of our brothers and sisters in the Christian community and beyond, particularly among the poor, the poor in spirit, and the sick. They are drawn from Jesus' parable about judgment day in which he states, "Just as you did it to the least of those who are members of my family, you did it to me" (Matthew 25:40).

- ❖ **Feed the hungry and give drink to the thirsty.**
  You might: Donate canned goods to a food pantry, help organize a food drive, volunteer at a soup kitchen, or prepare a meal each week for your family or a loved one.

207

Read Matthew
25:31–46 to find out
how important the
works of mercy are.

quick quote...

*In the end we will be
judged on love.*
—St. John
of the Cross

❖ **Clothe the naked.**

You might: Clean out your closet and donate to
the poor gently used clothes that don't fit or that
you don't wear anymore. Coordinate clothing,
coat or toiletries drives in your school or parish
or simply among friends and family.

❖ **Visit the sick.**

You might: Visit the sick in the hospital or prepare a meal for the family of someone who is ill.
Small gestures go a long way in spreading
Christ's love among the sick—and their care-
givers. Check your parish bulletin for the names
of the sick and send a get-well card even if you
don't know them. They will be comforted to
know that someone is praying for them. Offer to
prepare a meal, mow the lawn, or run errands for
them. Is there someone in your life who suffers
from depression, loneliness, or is under a lot of
stress? Send a "thinking-of-you" card or call to
get together.

❖ **Shelter the homeless.**

You might: Volunteer at a homeless shelter or
raise money for the sponsor organization. Welcome a stranger by learning about other cultures
so you can better relate to people of different eth-
nicities. Welcome new neighbors, get together
with them, and introduce them to your friends.

❖ **Visit the imprisoned.**

You might: Assist a prison minister or ministry, or
collect used books to donate to prisoners. Don't
forget those who may be prisoners in their
homes: the elderly, an overwhelmed new mom,
or a caregiver. Lend a helping hand, prepare a
meal, or pay a visit.

❖ **Bury the dead.**

You might: Attend wakes and funerals, pray for
the deceased, and have Masses said for them.
This will support their survivors.

Spiritual Works of Mercy are ways we come to the aid of our brothers and sisters in their spiritual needs. They may be a bit challenging to do but are important.

❖ **Admonish the sinner.**
   You might: Lovingly warn a friend or relative about the danger he or she is in because of sin. Invite someone to the sacrament of Reconciliation with you.

❖ **Instruct the ignorant.**
   You might: Teach in the religious education program at your parish, and share your faith through your words (written and oral) and deeds.

❖ **Counsel the doubtful.**
   You might: Help out in a social ministry that cares for confused and hurting people, and support your family and friends when they are in need of guidance and support.

❖ **Comfort the afflicted.**
   You might: Support those who have lost a loved one. Help address thank-you notes or take them to see a funny movie. Encourage them to spend time with friends. Around the holidays send a Christmas greeting or help with errands or household chores. Listen to stories or sit with those who grieve as they look through pictures. Cheer up those who are suffering any other kind of loss by writing them or talking to them with good news, support, advice and the promise of prayer.

❖ **Bear wrongs patiently.**
   You might: Refrain from taking revenge, or spreading the news of the injustice. Offer up your pain for a good intention.

❖ **Forgive injuries.**
   You might: Say "I forgive you." Treat the one

trivial tidbit...

Catholic Charities is the largest private network of social services in the United States. Check out its website at www. catholiccharitiesusa. org.

fyi...

In 1964, Jean Vanier founded the first lay community with and for people with developmental disabilities. Now there are more than one hundred L'Arche (The Ark) houses throughout the world where the members live and pray together.

In giving of our time to others, we often receive more than we ever give. Volunteering is rewarding and satisfying. What are your interests? Do you enjoy talking with people and finding out about their lives? Perhaps you could volunteer at a nursing home and through your companionship give comfort to someone who is lonely or sorrowful. Consider using a year of your life, even a few months, to carry out the works of mercy full-time or part-time. Use your gifts to help those in need. Each year the Catholic Network of Volunteer Service produces *Response: Directory of Volunteer Opportunities.* To get more information, visit www.cnvs.org.

who hurt you as though nothing ever happened. Try to rebuild your relationship.

❖ **Pray for the living and the dead.**
You might: Promise people you'll pray for them; then keep your promise. Offer general intercessions for people at Mass and other prayer services. Pray for others in your night prayers.

Duties of Catholics:
A Compass for Abundant Living
Here's a quick guide to helping you walk the talk—a compass for our duties as Catholics: the precepts of the Church. You can use this list to identify areas of your spiritual life that may need a little work.

1. **Observe the Lord's Day and holy days of obligation by participating in Mass and by resting.** We sanctify the day of the Lord's resurrection and principle feast days when we gather with other Catholics for the Eucharistic celebration. We also renew ourselves on these days by avoiding unnecessary work, such as business and shopping, and instead engage in activities to re-create ourselves.

2. **Celebrate the sacraments of Eucharist and Penance.** Minimally, we receive Communion at least once a year, preferably during the Easter season, and we confess grave sins at least once a year.

3. **Fast and abstain on the days appointed by the Church.** This prepares us to celebrate the feasts and gives us mastery over ourselves and freedom of heart.

4. **Provide for the needs of the Church.** We contribute to the support of the Church, not only our parish but the worldwide Church.

5. **Follow Church laws regarding marriage.** These are found in the Code of Canon Law. We also are responsible for seeing that our children receive religious training.
6. **Study Catholic teaching.** Our formation in the faith is ongoing; we strive to deepen our knowledge and understanding of God.
7. **Join in the work of the Church.** We act as missionaries and spread the Good News of Jesus to others. We also pray for all those in need throughout the world.

Supporting the Church means sharing your time, talent and treasure. Some people tithe, that is, they give one-tenth of their income to the Church. Others volunteer to mentor children in the faith or assist with any number of parish ministries. What can you do to share your time, talent or treasure with your church?

_____

_____

_____

With the poor? _____

_____

_____

Theological Virtues

There are three theological virtues infused at baptism that have to do with our relationship with God:

- ❖ Faith
- ❖ Hope
- ❖ Charity

quick quote...

The Christian ideal has not been tried and found wanting. It has been found difficult and left untried.

—G.K. Chesterton

fyi...

Catholic Relief Services (CRS) is the official overseas relief and development agency of the U.S. Catholic Church. CRS provides direct aid to the poor and involves people in their own development. In 2002, CRS reached sixty-two million people in ninety-one countries and territories, bringing relief in the wake of disasters and offering hope to the poor. Find out more about Catholic Relief Services at www. catholicrelief.org.

Cardinal Moral Virtues

"Cardinal" is from the word for "hinge." On these four virtues all other virtues are hinged. The cardinal virtues are the basis of moral life.

- ❖ Prudence
- ❖ Justice
- ❖ Fortitude
- ❖ Temperance

Capital Sins and Virtues

These seven capital sins are also known as "the seven deadly sins." They are the source of all other sins. For each vice, there is a parallel virtue that draws us closer to God:

Pride	Humility
Covetousness	Generosity
Lust	Chastity
Anger	Temperance
Envy	Brotherly Love
Sloth	Diligence
Gluttony	Moderation

Catholic Social Teaching

Perhaps one of the greatest strengths of our Catholic faith in the application of our ritual and belief is Catholic Social Teaching. As a Church, we commit not only to following Jesus in our spiritual life, but also in demanding justice in our world. Since Pope Leo XIII's encyclical *Rerum Novarum* ("On the Condition of Labor") in 1891, the Church has interpreted the teachings of Christ in the context of the world through writings called Catholic Social Teaching. The principles of Catholic Social Thought deal with the life and dignity of the human person; a call to family, community and participation; our rights and responsibilities as God's creation; support for the poor and vulnerable; the dignity of work and the rights of workers; solidarity; and care for God's creation. These themes supercede religious boundaries and extend into a moral obligation to defend the dignity of all human beings and our world.

Three principles included in these themes are solidarity, stewardship, and subsidiarity. *Solidarity* is union with the poor or victims of injustice. *Stewardship* is the attitude that God has entrusted us with gifts of creation to be shared with all. *Subsidiarity* means that social problems are solved at the lowest, closest, simplest level possible and that larger social organizations support smaller social organizations for the common good. This implies that leaders share their power and that everything is ordered for the good of the individual and not for the government.

Go in Peace to Love and Serve the Lord

Abundant living is the result of faithful living. We reach a full, rich life by our attempts to follow Jesus, humbling, flawed, and messy though they be. We try to live as Jesus did—full of love and compassion, forgiving others so that we receive his promise, "A good measure, pressed down, shaken together, running over, will be put into your lap" (Luke 6:38). We strive to do good so that we "may take hold of the life that really is life" (1 Timothy 6:19). Like Jesus, we carry our crosses—the hardships and suffering we face—in order to attain the new life he won for us. And in all these endeavors we fall and fail. In the end, abundant living is largely achieved not by a parade of the pious and perfect, but by a caravan of imperfect pilgrims seeking to come just a little closer to God with each step. This desire is why we Catholics do the rituals and disciplines and devotions and prayers in this book. They are the means to God's grace and power, which are ours for the

A virtuous life is simply impossible without the aid of prayer.
—St. John Chrysostom

213

There may be times when we are power-less to prevent injustice, but there must never be a time when we fail to protest it.

—Elie Wiesel

asking and which make it possible to experience life to the full here as well as eternal life. By spending time with Jesus, reading the Gospels to get to know him better, and by asking "What would Jesus do?" (WWJD), we not only guarantee abundant life for ourselves but we also become Christ in the world today, conduits of his love and life for others. We walk the path toward abundant life by choosing to live abundantly in Christ, who said, "I am the way, the truth and life."

On Blessed Mother Teresa of Calcutta's business card:
The fruit of silence is PRAYER.
The fruit of prayer is FAITH.
The fruit of faith is LOVE.
The fruit of love is SERVICE.
The fruit of service is PEACE.

Acknowledgements

Every effort has been made to trace and acknowledge copyright holders of the prayers included in this work. We apologize for any errors or omissions that may remain and invite those concerned to contact the publishers, who will ensure that full acknowledgement is made in the future.

In gratitude to Carolyn Joyce Carty, for contributing her poem, *Footprints*. (Additional information about her work is available at http://faithweb2.tripod.com.)

Index of Prayers

The Confirmed Catholic's Prayer Journal

_____

_____

_____

_____

_____

_____

_____

_____

_____

_____

_____

_____

_____

_____

_____

_____

_____

The Confirmed Catholic's Prayer Journal

The Confirmed Catholic's Prayer Journal